Oregon Wine Country

John Doerper

Photography by Greg Vaughn

COMPASS AMERICAN GUIDES
An imprint of Fodor's Travel Publications

Compass American Guides: Oregon Wine Country

Editor: Craig Seligman
Designer: Tina R. Malaney
Compass Editorial Director: Daniel Mangin
Compass Creative Director: Fabrizio La Rocca
Compass Senior Editor: Kristin Moehlmann
Production Editor: David Downing
Photo Editor and Archival Researcher: Melanie Marin
Map Design: Mark Stroud, Moon Street Cartography

Cover photo (Bear Creek Winery) by Greg Vaughn

The details in this book are based on information supplied to us at press time, but changes
occur all the time, and the publisher cannot accept responsibility for facts that become outdated
or for inadvertent errors or omissions.

First Edition
ISBN 1–4000–1367–4
ISSN 1547–8726

Compass American Guides, 1745 Broadway, New York, NY 10019
PRINTED IN SINGAPORE

10 9 8 7 6 5 4 3 2 1

To Victoria—who really knows wine.

C O N T E N T S

Topical Essays and Sidebars

Maps

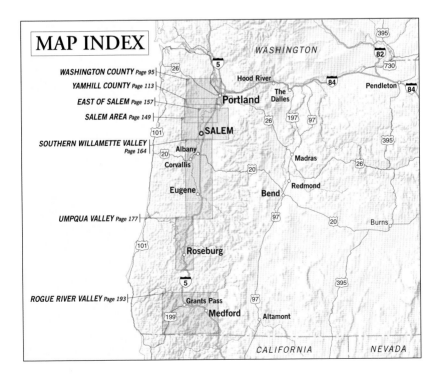

MAP INDEX

WASHINGTON

Hood River
The Dalles
Portland
Pendleton

SALEM

Albany
Corvallis
Madras

Eugene
Redmond
Bend

Burns

Roseburg

Grants Pass
Medford
Altamont

CALIFORNIA   NEVADA

INTRODUCTION

■ A Wine Country Idyll

THE PICNIC WAS A DELIGHT. We stopped at a winery and picked up a chilled bottle of pinot gris, made our way to a picnic table overlooking a fragrant meadow, and unpacked our sandwiches, fruit, and cheese. To the east rose the sharply pointed peak of Mount Jefferson, white against the sky. Goldfinches kept us company, darting from thistle to thistle. They ignored the red-tailed hawk circling overhead. So did the skein of geese flying south on strong wings, honking as they passed.

When we finished, we noticed something moving on the surface of the pond below and decided to investigate. A trail wound down to the reedy shore. Tall alders, their branches intertwined with the large-leaved vines of the wild cucumber Marah, threw a soft shade onto cattails bending in the breeze. Out in the water, a blocky creature began to move in widening circles. It surveyed us apprehensively and apparently didn't like what it saw. Up came a big, flat tail, and then it hit the water with a loud *slap!* The beaver cruised to the far side of the pond. *Splash!* Its tail struck the water again, sending concentric ripples out over the water's calm surface.

We ignored him; there wasn't much else we could do. We couldn't entice him with food (beavers eat bark), the way we'd bribed the shrub jay that darted out of the woods to harass us until we soothed its temper with a crust of bread. The beaver soon quieted down and returned to the shadows. A western meadowlark gurgled flutelike notes at the grassy verge, and below us, from the cattails, came the buzzing trill of a marsh wren. The breeze carried an aroma of moist reeds, drying hay, and the freshly squeezed grape juice known as must—the harvest had begun. Soon the new wine would be fermenting in vats, its enticing aromas wafting through dry oak woods, moist meadows, and shady draws.

We returned to our table, took a final sip of wine, and walked back to the winery. Earlier, it had been quiet; now it bustled. Trucks hauled in gondolas of grapes, to be weighed and then dumped into a stemmer-crusher. The machine would then free the fruit from its stems and crack the skins so the juice could flow into waiting vats.

That evening, we sat by the open window of a room overlooking the Pacific Ocean. Our inn was a short drive from the vineyards, allowing us to savor the best of the Oregon autumn—a warm day among the vines, a cool evening on the beach, a dinner of fresh local shrimp and salmon. We sipped a glorious late-harvest Riesling and gazed out at the gray whales frolicking just beyond the surf.

(preceding pages) Light glimmers through wine bottles, and (pages 10–11) a Yamhill County vineyard. (opposite) Washington County hills and vineyards, the perfect setting for a picnic.

Crushing grapes the old-fashioned way—efficient, but messy.

■ Four Decades of Change

Our Wine Country idyll reminded me just how much change has occurred in Oregon in the four decades since I first tasted the state's wines. In the 1970s, there were only few wineries, tucked into the hills far from sight. If you managed to find one, and to find a wine you liked there, you were lucky if you could buy a bottle to take home, because production was limited. Although the same conditions hold true today for a few rarified wineries, by the early 1980s a perceptible transformation was under way. More vineyards were being planted, and more wineries had opened to the public. Wine touring, with Portland, Eugene, or Ashland as a base, was evolving into a popular weekend pursuit.

In those early days, many wineries remained mostly or completely closed to the public. Today only a few are still off limits, though even they tend to open once or twice a year, usually on Memorial Day and Thanksgiving Day weekends. On those special occasions, they go all out, releasing rare wines, matching their wines with delectable foods prepared by well-known local chefs, and even providing musical entertainment.

■ ENTHUSIASTIC SUPPORT

Oregon wineries generally welcome everyone with an interest in fine wine. The camaraderie between visitors and staff may run deeper here than anywhere else in the West, if only because enophiles here recall how difficult it was to get a local wine industry up and running. The state had a few wineries before Prohibition, but they didn't survive the era, and new ones didn't begin to thrive until the wine boom of the 1960s and 1970s. During those decades, innovative California wine-makers moved north in search of vineyards where cool-climate grapes would do well. And Oregon wine buffs, to their credit, rallied round the new wineries even before their wines had become truly exceptional. Now that some Oregon wines rank among the best in the world, the support is as enthusiastic as ever.

In typically Oregonian style, though, this support stops short of fanaticism— and short of chauvinism too. No event better expresses the easygoing spirit of the Northwest wine community than the **International Pinot Noir Celebration,** held in late July in McMinnville, in the heart of the Yamhill County vineyards. Anyone lucky enough to score a ticket can mingle with winemakers from as far afield as France, Italy, Australia, and New Zealand, all of whom have one thing in common: they grow and vinify pinot noir. One year, I listened to a group of French wine-makers sniff that Oregon pinot noirs are too heavy on oak and too light on finesse. An Oregon winemaker at our table smiled calmly and told them to be patient: in a few years the state's wineries had made remarkable strides with their pinot noirs, and they had every intention—and every prospect—of making greater ones.

The International Pinot Noir Celebration, held on the campus of the otherwise teetotaling Linfield College, mixes serious lectures and tastings with the kind of laid-back outdoor activities that have earned it a reputation as a summer camp for adults. The less-restrained activities center around food and wine (of course) and terminate with a spectacular barbecue in which chefs grill local salmon, Native American fashion, on alder sticks propped over a large oak fire. Postprandial activi-ties vary from an all-night kegger on campus to spirited dancing at Nick's Italian Cafe downtown. Some enophiles who can't make it to the big events purchase tick-ets for the Afternoon of Pinot Noir, on Sunday, the event's concluding day. At a recent tasting, five dozen pinot noirs from around the globe partnered dishes pre-pared by seven of Portland's hottest new chefs. *International Pinot Noir Celebration; 503-472-8964.*

■ CLOUDS ON THE HORIZON, ENCOURAGING SIGNS

As the reputations of Oregon's wines have grown, so have their prices. The state's new wine aficionados now clamor for local vintages, but unfortunately their knowledge doesn't always match their understandable pride. And often they're further confused by writers so excited to have local wineries to cover that their boosterism outstrips their judgment. And so I've written this guide to provide not just connoisseurs but also beginners with solid tips on tasting and purchasing Oregon wines—the best of which, as I've said, now rank with the best made anywhere in the world.

Yet there are a few clouds on the horizon. Oregon's wines are improving as both competition and consumer sophistication increase, but I find myself developing concern about Oregon's signature wine, pinot noir. Heretical as it may be to say this, the future of Oregon wine may lie less in the well-publicized vineyards of the Northern Willamette Valley (so convenient to metropolitan Portland and Salem) than in those of the remote valleys of southern Oregon, where the state's post-Prohibition wine industry restarted back in the early 1960s, before the newer northerly wineries eclipsed them.

During the past three decades, Oregon has staked its good name on pinot noir and chardonnay, but—and this opinion could get me roasted over a fire of vine clippings and barrel staves—they may not be its best grapes. True, Oregon pinot noirs generally range from very good to excellent. But they rarely break into the class of the French red burgundies they're attempting to emulate. Many California pinot noirs—notably those from the Santa Rita Hills and the Russian River Valley—are more exciting and boast more varietal character. Pinot noirs from both states can achieve greatness, but the California bottlings achieve it more often. I feel the same way about chardonnay. Granted, some people have blamed that grape's inferior performance in Oregon—with some justice, perhaps—on an inferior clone planted in the state's vineyards years ago. The situation will soon be remedied, we're told, with new plantings, which are just starting to produce superior grapes. I hope that indeed is what happens. We'll have to wait and see.

Meanwhile, though, encouraging signs abound. Oregon excels, in the cool vineyards of the north, with pinot gris, an Alsatian white-wine grape; with pinot blanc, chardonnay's less illustrious Burgundian cousin; and with German Riesling. In the warm vineyards of southern Oregon's Umpqua and Rogue River Valleys, the stars are red Bordeaux varieties—cabernet sauvignon, merlot, malbec—and new plantings of syrah and tempranillo. Young wineries and new varieties bring happy

Comparing notes at the International Pinot Noir Celebration, an alfresco summer event that takes place on the campus of Linfield College in McMinnville.

surprises with every vintage. And as more and more visitors vacation in the wine valleys, new restaurants and inns spring up to cater to their needs. Because both the Wine-Country landscape and many Oregon wines are still little known to visitors, this is a perfect region for travelers who love exploring new ground but have no interest in leaving comfort behind.

When it's great, wine is more than just another beverage. To fully understand it, you need to know its background and something about the people who create it. And so I'm inviting you on a tour of a place where some of the world's most delicious wines are produced in some of the world's most beautiful settings. I'll give you a short history of the region and fill you in on the (often eccentric) men and women who grow the grapes and make the wines, and I won't forget the foods and the chefs that have put Oregon onto the nation's culinary map. This book has a dual purpose: as a guidebook for the wine traveler, and as an excursion for the armchair traveler who has just poured a glass of good wine and is settling back now, ready to read.

Pinot noir leaves in the autumn, when the fruit is ready for harvest.

THE SETTING

■ THREE-IN-ONE WINE COUNTRY

WINE CAME LATE TO OREGON. Not until the late 20th century were there enough premium wineries here to warrant a special trip. But those that did exist became popular early on, when they were few and scattered, because there were always plenty of other things to do nearby—and that remains so today. There are covered bridges to view, lazy rivers down which you can float on an inner tube, and swift streams on which adventurous rafters brave whitewater torrents. There are small towns to explore, with their ubiquitous antiques shops; farmers' markets to visit; and museums where you can learn about local history. You can fish for trout and salmon. On a hot day, after you've tasted all the wine you desire, the cool meadows of the Cascade Mountains or the breezy coastal beaches are but a short drive away.

The Cascades, a volcanic chain east of the Wine Country, and the densely wooded Coast Range, rising to the west, protect it from extreme weather, creating a climate perfect for the production of wine grapes. But, really, there is more than just one Oregon Wine Country. There are three adjacent wine regions between the two ranges, and each of the three can be divided into significant subregions.

Many Willamette Valley visitors combine winery touring with antiquing.

The Southern Willamette Valley's Coyote Creek Covered Bridge.

■ WILLAMETTE VALLEY

Oregon's three major wine regions lie in the western part of the state, and the largest vineyard area is the northernmost, the Willamette Valley—that is, the valley of the Willamette River. The oak-studded valley falls into two basins, northern and southern, set off from each other by hills and smaller river valleys. The Willamette Valley received heavy loads of silt during the huge Spokane Floods 19,000 years ago, making its bottom soils similar to those of the Columbia, Yakima, and Walla Walla Valleys, which were also flooded at that time. But the soils of the tributary valleys and of the hillsides are different, attesting to a long and complex geologic history. And because the Willamette Valley is so diverse geographically, it has myriad microclimates—one, it sometimes seems, that's right for every variety of grape.

The subregions, moving from north to south, include the Valley of the Tualatin, tucked between the Tualatin and the Chehalem Mountains, west and southwest of Portland; the valley of the Yamhill River, between the Chehalem Mountains and the Amity Hills; the Eola Hills and the South Salem Hills, west and south of Salem; and the southern Willamette Valley, near Eugene. Some of the vineyards of the latter region are in the Valley proper, but most are in the hills to the south, which are part of the Coast Range and are drained by the Siuslaw River and its tributaries.

Most of the Willamette Valley's wineries are in the north (in the Eola and Amity Hills and in the Yamhill and Tualatin River Valleys), near Portland and its suburbs, where an influx of computer and software companies has created an intellectual climate—and a consumer climate—similar to those of California's Silicon Valley. But there are also wineries near Salem, the state capital, and near the university towns of Corvallis (home of Oregon State University) and Eugene (the University of Oregon).

The Willamette Valley ends south of Eugene, where the Coast Range bumps into the Western Cascades, leaving just enough room for the Coast Fork of the Willamette River. The landscape changes visibly as you head south. Interstate 5 runs in a flat, straight line through the southern Willamette Valley (its flattest section), then begins to climb as it crosses the Willamette River in south Eugene. For the rest of the way, until you hit the state line, the four-lane freeway curves and winds over hills and through river valleys.

Ready for the crush: grape pickers harvest Riesling from vines in Yamhill County.

■ UMPQUA VALLEY

Oregon's second important wine region, the Umpqua Valley, lies south of the Willamette Valley, its borders the Umpqua River and its south fork, the South Umpqua. This pastoral landscape of forests, meadows and mountains contains so many valleys the area is known as the Hundred Valleys of the Umpqua. Rugged mountains squeeze the North Umpqua, while the South Umpqua curves its way through gentle valleys that are bathed in sunshine for much of the year. This is where most of the vineyards and wineries are; a few lie farther west, on the cool slopes of the main Umpqua near Elkton.

The Umpqua's north and south forks join into the main river north of Roseburg, at an elevation so low that it's almost down to sea level—yet the Umpqua still must traverse most of the Coast Range to reach the ocean. It does so at the same low elevation, making it the only navigable coastal river between the Columbia to the north and the Sacramento to the south. The head of tidewater is at Scottsburg, halfway down the Coast Range; in the 19th century, steamboats chugged upriver as far as Roseburg. Below Scottsburg, the placid Umpqua looks more like a fjord than a river. This deep cut in the Coast Range is a boon to grape growers. In the summer, cool air penetrates far inland, lowering the temperature in the valleys enough to allow cool-climate grapes to thrive; meanwhile, cabernet and zinfandel ripen on the higher, warmer slopes. In winter, the low valleys siphon off cold air that might otherwise harm the vines.

The mountains surrounding Roseburg are a transitional area between Oregon and California. Here representative rocks and plants from both regions mingle. This goes for grapevines too: cool-climate grapes, such as Riesling, thrive here as comfortably as such warm-climate varieties as cabernet sauvignon and tempranillo. Roseburg is also the cultural center of the Umpqua Valley, with easy-to-reach restaurants, hotels, and shops.

■ ROGUE RIVER VALLEY

Oregon's southernmost wine region, the Rogue River Valley, is one of the oldest and by far the most rugged of the Pacific Northwest's grape-growing areas. Large stretches of the Rogue River flow between walls so steep that they allow access to the river only by jet boat. But in the Medford–Grants Pass–Cave Junction region,

The rustic Applegate Valley setting of Valley View Vineyards, overlooked by the Siskiyou Mountains deep in the Rogue River Valley.

subsidiary valleys widen enough to support orchards and vineyards. The Rogue and its tributaries, Bear Creek and the Applegate and Illinois Rivers, lie just a few miles from California, and the weather here is much warmer than even in the Umpqua Valley vineyards. The native vegetation, running heavily to pines as well as ceanothus, manzanita, and other chaparral plants, suggests a world apart from the more northerly wine regions, and the wines too have a character of their own. Rogue River Valley cabernet sauvignon is spicier than California's, and the higher-elevation vineyards produce excellent pinot noir and pinot gris. Ashland, with its theaters and its renowned Oregon Shakespeare Festival, is the region's cultural center, with excellent inns and restaurants but only a couple of wineries—though the slopes of the nearby Bear Creek Valley, once famous for pears, are now home to some superior vineyards.

■ BEYOND THE WINE COUNTRY

Eastern Oregon also has vineyards, most notably in the Hood River Valley, in and around Boardman. These vineyards are in the Columbia Valley American Viticultural Area (AVA), a federally designated grape-growing region, or appellation, that lies mostly to the north, in Washington. There are also vineyards in the Milton-Freewater region (part of the Walla Walla Valley AVA), and also mostly in Washington. But Eastern Oregon has only a few wineries, small ones in the Hood River section of the Columbia Gorge, so our concentration here will be on the wineries of the Willamette, Umpqua, and Rogue River Valleys.

Harvesting grapes by hand outside Jacksonville in southern Oregon, ca. 1907.

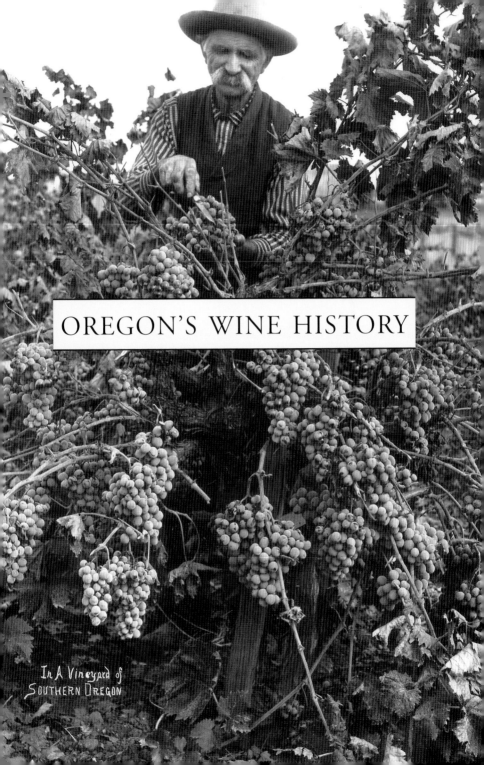

OREGON'S WINE HISTORY

In A Vineyard of
Southern Oregon

■ A DEEP LOVE OF WINE

THE SMALL CHAMPOEG WINE CELLARS huddles below evenly spaced rows of grapevines—they run up a gentle slope almost to the crown of the hill known as La Butte, where they end at a grove of Douglas firs—and the road below. Native camas lilies bedeck flower boxes with blue blossoms; a huge Oregon oak shades a small picnic area in a lush meadow. It's a scene like many others in Oregon Wine Country, yet it's special, because this is pioneer country. Here, overlooking French Prairie, and across the Willamette River near present-day Newberg, settlers first laid out their farms back in the 1830s, making the Willamette Valley the West Coast region longest settled by English-speaking Americans.

But the French came first—French-Canadians, that is, who spoke the patois that served as the lingua franca of the Hudson's Bay Company, the huge British monopoly that controlled the fur trade in the Pacific Northwest. In 1847, Judge John W. Grim listened to a speech by the Hudson's Bay Company's Tom McKay, who was raising troops to avenge the massacre of the missionary Marcus Whitman and his family by Cayuse Indians. According to S. A. Clarke in "Pioneers of Oregon," a December 1884 story in *Overland Monthly and Out West* magazine, what most impressed the judge was not McKay's eloquence but the fact that his speech was

> addressed to different groups in different languages. The Americans
> heard from him pure English; to the Canadians he spoke French;
> and the half-castes listened to eloquent passages in the Chinook jar-
> gon common to all classes. He involuntarily changed from one to
> another tongue; and whatever language he used, his words were
> effectual and impressive. It was a scene that surprised the new-comer,
> though not inconsistent with those early times.

The French-Canadians had journeyed over from eastern Canada, paddling huge Hudson's Bay Company cargo canoes; after years of service, they had retired to the shores of the Willamette and started farms. English-speaking settlers from the American Midwest arrived by wagon, and so-called mountain men, weary of the dangerous trapper's life, settled here too. But it was the French-Canadians who brought the deepest love of food and, especially, wine. They settled on a slope

Many decades before the wine boom, a 1911 promotional booklet celebrates Oregon grapes.

GRANT'S PASS AND JOSEPHINE COUNTY

ROGUE RIVER VALLEY
OREGON

above the Willamette (where their pioneer cemetery still lies beneath shady trees), built homes, plowed fields, and planted vineyards—on the very slope of La Butte that Champoeg Wine Cellars occupies today. When the winery's owners began planting in the early 1970s, they found old pinot meunier grapes growing here, survivors from vineyards dating all the way back to the 1840s. An 1880 farm report referred to the neighboring community of Butteville as the wine capital of the Oregon Territory.

A short distance upriver, Oregon history took a major turn. Great Britain, through the Hudson's Bay Company, had long held claim to the territory. But in 1843, the settlers—the majority of whom were still French-Canadian—held Oregon's first constitutional meeting, for the purpose of establishing a provisional American government. From then on, Oregon paid allegiance to the United States. Today, the site of the convention is the popular **Champoeg State Park,** with picnic areas and woodland trails.

The surrounding landscape has changed much since pioneer days. Where prairies once spread between the clumps of trees dotting the valley floor to the north and south of the Willamette, fields now alternate with pastures. Deciduous trees still mark the course of the river and cloak the ridges and knolls that break up the valley floor. To the east and west, dense forests of conifers march up the foothills of the Cascades and the Coast Range.

The retired French-Canadian trappers weren't the first settlers to plant grapes in the Oregon Territory. The British planted grape seeds from England at Fort Vancouver shortly after the fort's establishment in 1824–25, augmenting them with vines brought over from Europe. The Hudson's Bay Company founded the fort as a trading depot in what is now Washington State, on the northern bank of the Columbia River near its confluence with the Willamette. Official records show that wine was served at Fort Vancouver's formal meals, but Chief Factor John McLoughlin had no taste for it and discouraged its use with quotidian meals. The grapes from the fort's vineyards were probably enjoyed as fresh fruit instead of being vinified. The Protestant missionary Narcissa Whitman, visiting Fort Vancouver in 1836, wrote of plucking fruit from the arbor at the chief factor's house: "The grapes are just ripe and I am feasting on them finely."

(above) Pinot gris grapes, ripe on the vine and ready for plucking. (below) A fine Oregon apple harvest, ca. 1910.

■ SPORADIC PROGRESS

Beginning around 1840, black-robed padres taught Native Americans north of the Columbia River agriculture and the Gospels—and made wine for religious services and for themselves. To the south, the Mexican War had welded California to the Union, and that state's gold rush strengthened those ties, improving transportation and bringing new settlers, some of whom, having learned winemaking in the old country, arrived with grapevines and helped establish the California wine industry.

In Oregon, although grapes were grown from the earliest pioneer days, winemaking has had a sporadic history. Most of our information comes from anecdotes that can't always be fully verified, but we do know that pioneer vintners and gardeners understood that the region was hospitable to grapes. The soils were lean and well drained; the climate was mild, with the warm days and cool nights that foster sweetness and acidity in the grapes; and rainfall was ample. This was a land where a budding vintner could stick cuttings into the ground and, with minimal care, watch them sprout and produce superior grapes.

That's exactly what the pioneer vintners did—Old World winemakers turned those grapes into excellent wines. Immigrant coopers made vats and barrels for aging and fermenting the wines. And yet, after some initial triumphs, the Oregon wine industry languished. The reasons were cultural rather than agricultural: though the French-Canadian trappers and the European immigrants loved wine with their meals, the Midwestern farmers who soon became the majority settlers did not. Nor did the Scandinavian loggers and fishermen who came later. They preferred beer and whiskey; if they drank wine at all, it had to be strong stuff, and that kind of wine could be made more easily from apples and berries than from grapes. Still, grape growing and winemaking never quite vanished from the region. A few wineries hung on, making wines mainly for settlers of German, French, Italian, and Balkan ancestry, and providing grapes for those, like the retired trappers, who preferred to make their own. But most of the wine consumed in Oregon's pioneer homes was either homemade or imported from Europe or California.

The first native American grape variety in the Northwest appears to have been Isabella, a New York wine grape that arrived from the Midwest, via the Oregon Trail, in 1847. But it had little impact on local plantings, since by that time mission grapevines from California had become well established at Fort Vancouver and in the Willamette Valley. In 1854, Peter Britt, a noted photographer, planted a vineyard near Jacksonville, in southern Oregon's Rogue River Valley. A decade later a winery followed, and soon other immigrants began to plant vineyards and establish wineries in the Umpqua and Rogue River Valleys. It took longer for grapes to reach the Tualatin Valley, but by the end of the 19th century a German immigrant named Reuter (sometimes spelled Rueter) had planted a vineyard and opened a winery (apparently an award-winning one) on David Hill, near Forest Grove.

By 1859, the American population of Oregon had grown large enough for the territory to earn statehood. But Oregon's fledgling wine industry, even once it was established in the Applegate, Umpqua, and Tualatin Valleys, received little attention from the state's gourmets, perhaps because cosmopolitan Portland had such easy access to first-rate European wines. In *Delights and Prejudices,* his autobiographical paean to good eating, Oregon's most famous epicure, the late James Beard, barely mentions local wine when describing his mother's table, one of the most sumptuously appointed in the West. Oregon wine makes a brief appearance early in the book, when Beard describes his mother's special relationship with an Italian-born truck gardener who supplied her household with fresh produce: "He was not long in falling under the wily spell of Mother and would bring her choice tidbits, bottles of homemade wine and sometimes Italian dishes made by his wife."

Harvesting wheat in 19th-century Yamhill County; many fields here today are planted to grapes.

■ From Prohibition to the Boom

Unlike California, where some wineries made fortunes during the "Great Experiment" known as Prohibition, Oregon saw its wine industry virtually shut down, and the situation hardly improved following repeal. For a short period during the 1930s, "farm wineries" (most of them making fruit wines) flourished, and they did well again during World War II, when alcohol in any form was in high demand. But the Northwest lacked creative entrepreneurs like the McCreas and the Davies, who so improved the quality of California wines; nor did the region have wine dynasties like California's Gallos, Martinis, Mondavis, and Pedroncellis. The prominent West Coast food writer Helen Evans Brown dismissed Oregon wines in her 1952 *West Coast Cook Book*. "When I speak of our wines, I mean Californian. The amount produced in Oregon . . . is negligible."

In the meantime, though, home winemakers were turning out a great deal of wine (from grapes as well as other fruits). They did so well into the second half of the 20th century—developing skills that, when the time was right, would precipitate Oregon's wine revolution. Most of these home winemakers were of Mediterranean ancestry, raised in cultures that valued wine as a vital part of every meal. In his 1997 book about early Oregon winemakers, *The Boys Up North*, the Portland writer Paul Pintarich remembers his Croatian grandfather's growing grapes in his Portland backyard, from which every fall the old man would make his own wine. When Pintarich mentioned this wine years later, his father told him, "Your grandpa made terrible wine. And he made it out of everything, even Grandma's grape jam. And he bottled it in any kind of containers he could find, even old syrup bottles." Fortunately, we can assume that not all homemade wine was quite so wretched, because several home winemakers went on to open successful wineries.

The development of a professional wine industry continued to elude Oregonians well into the 20th century. "There was a time, in the not-so-distant past," the former *Seattle Times* wine columnist Tom Stockley wrote in his 1978 book *Winery Tours in Oregon, Washington, Idaho, and British Columbia*, "when wines of the Pacific Northwest were, to put it mildly, laughable." But then, Stockley continued, "the wine boom hit." Northwestern wines took off in the 1970s—owing much of their success to the booming California wine industry,

A wine hero: Peter Britt, seen here with his camera, photographed grapes and, beginning in 1854, cultivated them.

which supplied not just know-how but winemakers as well. It was only after a group of young Californians, fresh out of university, started making vinifera wines in the Umpqua Valley and the Willamette Valley in the 1960s and 1970s—and gained international acclaim for them—that Oregon's wines became fashionable.

A few of the state's present-day wine boosters are so enthusiastic that they can talk themselves out of noticing any flaws; but the truth is that Oregon has very little really bad wine. Unlike California and Washington, Oregon currently produces no bulk wine, perhaps because the state has no large corporate wineries; even its two largest, King Estate and Willamette Valley, are small in comparison with the huge wine empires that operate in California and Washington. Oregon's industry is, happily, still largely dominated by family and boutique wineries, and many of their best wines aren't for sale outside the state beyond a specialty wine shop here and there. That's why it's imperative for connoisseurs to explore Oregon Wine Country on their own and taste these wines at the source.

At Oregon's best restaurants, the food, made of fresh ingredients and fancifully presented, enhances the wine—and vice versa.

FOOD AND WINE

■ AN ENDLESS BOUNTY

THE THREE OREGON VALLEYS now celebrated for their wine have been producing excellent foods for more than a century: beef, chicken, lamb, crayfish, salmon, shad, trout, cheese, apples, berries, pears, hazelnuts, walnuts, and wild mushrooms. Over the past two decades, local chefs have been matching these foods to local wines with delectable results. Though their style of cooking is often called Northwest, these chefs tend to draw their inspiration from New York, France, and elsewhere in Europe rather than from Washington (or California).

As Oregon developed a wine industry of its own, the state's new winemakers planted much the same grapes that had proved their compatibility with food in France and California, and to a lesser degree in Germany and Italy—but with a difference in emphasis. They planted the vineyards in southern Oregon with traditional Bordeaux grapes, such as cabernet sauvignon and merlot. The vineyards of northern Oregon went to the traditional grapes of Burgundy and Alsace: chardonnay, pinot noir, and, to a lesser extent, pinot blanc and pinot gris. These choices weren't just a matter of climate. They were also a reaction to culinary preferences: southern Oregon is beef country; in northern Oregon lighter meats and seafood hold sway.

Oregon chefs inherited a European tradition of matching food and wine, and some partnerships were longstanding and obvious: beef with cabernet sauvignon or pinot noir; lamb with syrah; oysters with chardonnay or sauvignon blanc. But they made two discoveries that amounted to revelations. Both Oregon pinot gris and Oregon pinot noir pair beautifully with salmon. And, surprisingly, the pinot noir also enhances mussel dishes and, perhaps because of its relatively high acid content, holds up nicely against other seafood dishes as well. Matching wines with individual dishes can be a complicated matter when it comes to honoring both tradition and personal taste. But some rules are really just prejudices. Purists might frown upon serving a big Riesling with beef, but that's a common match in France's Alsace region. They might frown upon serving red wine with fish, but that's traditionally done in French red-wine regions, where—as in *filets de soles à la bordelaise* and *truites en vin rouge*—the fish isn't only accompanied by red wine but also cooked in it.

Still, some Oregon dishes can be tricky to pair with the proper wine. The obvious choice for a dish of spareribs cooked in blackberry wine might be the wine the ribs were cooked in—if you feel like drinking blackberry wine. But you might find they go even better with a pinot noir, a dolcetto, or a tempranillo; it all depends on the dominant flavors of the dish and of the bottle. Only an actual tasting will tell.

Because Oregon's wine industry flowered at the very moment that a new food and wine consciousness was sweeping the country, the area's wines were created with food in mind right from the beginning. The 1980s and 1990s were a highly creative period in regional cookery, but these years also saw a return to traditional dishes based on the freshest products from garden, farm, river, and sea. Oregonians love smoked foods (a cooking method they inherited from the region's Native Americans), and they smoke not only hams, sausages, beef, and salmon but also clams, sturgeon, and even hazelnuts. (Oregon grows some 90 percent of the nation's hazelnuts, and the nuts turn up in all kinds of dishes, from hazelnut pasta to hazelnut cookies.)

The state's many rivers and its long coastline supply fresh rockfish, salmon, smelt, sturgeon, clams, crabs, crayfish, mussels, oysters, and shrimp. Though salmon isn't as ubiquitous as it once was, both fresh and smoked salmon are still plentiful, with the best smoked salmon coming from small smokehouses in such fishing-port towns as Astoria, Garibaldi, Charleston, and Port Orford. In the ocean

Oregon chinook salmon with mushroom duxelles, at the Joel Palmer House in Dayton—where mushrooms rule.

The great James Beard, an Oregonian who did much to raise the standards of American cooks.

ports, you can also find excellent fresh albacore (in season) and smoked albacore, as well as fresh and smoked halibut. Oysters and scallops come fresh and smoked too. Another fish that's delectable when smoked is the richly flavored, almost oily sablefish—usually sold as black cod, though it's not even distantly related to the cods. All this seafood is delicious, and all varieties go very well with most chardonnay, dry Riesling, pinot gris, and even viognier.

James Beard praised Oregon seafood in his 1964 *Delights and Prejudices*. Enumerating the fish and shellfish available to his family during its annual sojourn at the beach, he singled out two local specialties:

> The Pacific's greatest blessing, though, was the Dungeness crab, to my mind unequalled by anything in the shellfish world. (I will match a good Dungeness against the best lobster in America and the best *langouste* in Europe.) In addition to the crab, there were the superb razor clams . . . . These flourished in the days of our beaching and continue in small supply nowadays—definitely a sportsman's catch. They have a rich flavor, somewhat akin to scallops, and a delicacy of texture that is different from any other clam I know.

Beard was more ambivalent about another seafood: "Small amounts of home-style [sturgeon] caviar were done as well—some of it thoroughly delicious and the rest undistinguished." That's still the case today.

The state's vast rangelands provide beef and lamb. Its dairy farms produce excellent milk and cream, which once supported a great number of cheese makers, from Pistol River in the south to Tillamook in the north. Most of the original producers vanished long ago, but the famed cheddars of Tillamook and Bandon are still being made; so are Oregon blue from Central Point and a superb newcomer, a camembert made by Oregon Gourmet Cheeses, a tiny dairy in Albany.

Orchards in the Bear Creek and Hood River Valleys produce abundant apples, cherries, and pears. The dark red Bing cherry was first bred in a Portland-area garden, and Oregon is one of the few places in the world where fragrant Comice pears, so lusciously soft they can be eaten with a spoon, are still grown commercially. The Willamette Valley produces flavorful blackberries, raspberries, and strawberries, as well as Oregon's signature berry, the delicious marionberry. Every year large crops of savory wild huckleberries ripen in Coast Range and Cascade Mountain forests.

Oregon's rabbit and farm-raised quail are also excellent. The state abounds in venison and game birds, but those meats are rarely available to visitors. (If you're lucky enough to get invited to a venison dinner, bring a big cabernet sauvignon or syrah for your hosts.)

Wine Country restaurants pride themselves on serving the freshest local vegetables, notably tiny "new" Yukon gold and red potatoes, broccoli, cauliflower, sweet and sugar snap peas, corn, vine-ripened tomatoes, and chili peppers. Northwest beets and leeks are in a class by themselves. Artichokes are grown commercially on the coast. Wild vegetables, often gathered by professional collectors, include various kelps ("ocean salad"), pickleweed and other wild greens, and mushrooms, most commonly chanterelles and morels. Many of these fruits and vegetables go surprisingly well with local wines: asparagus and artichokes with sémillon and sauvignon blanc, wild mushrooms with Northwest reds, kelp with chardonnay. A touch of Riesling improves apples, melons, peaches, pears, and strawberries; muscat does marvels for apricots and berries. Cherries and pinot noir are a delightful match.

■ PROMOTIONAL TOOLS

Oregon's winemakers have gone to great lengths to promote their wines as partners for Oregon foods—they never seem to tire of demonstrating the affinity of the state's pinot noirs for its salmon. Winemaker dinners have become a popular marketing tool, and no wonder: consumers get to enjoy superb meals in which each course has been carefully matched to a wine; winemakers get to show off their wares with foods specially designed by master chefs to bring out a vintage's best, virtually guaranteeing increased sales; and chefs get to show what they can do when they're inspired by a special wine. Even the youngest, least-established wineries are jumping into the game, drafting various staffers (often the winemaker's spouse) to prepare regional menus. Larger wineries hire professional chefs for these chores; a few even keep a full-time chef. (One unintended consequence of winemaker dinners is that for some participants they reinforce the widely held assumption that a wine is great only when it can hold its own against food. There's some old-fashioned puritanism behind the idea that a wine that earns its place at the table is somehow more praiseworthy than a wine consumed on its own.)

(opposite) Except for the kittens, a cross-section of Oregon's agricultural bounty.
(following pages) Corks from around the state at Nick's Italian Cafe in McMinnville.

The winemakers' other great promotional tool is on the bottles itself: a back label that often carries recommendations as to which foods the wine most enhances, and vice versa. There tends to be a lot of flexibility in these recommendations. Yamhill County's Amity tells us that its Eco Wine pinot noir is "ideal for pastas, grilled fish, chicken, and picnic fare"; its pinot blanc goes with "traditional Chardonnay dishes such as veal, or traditionally dry Riesling dishes such as scallops." Table Rock hawks its pinot blanc as an "excellent companion to trout, steelhead, or crab." Chateau Benoit recommends its Müller-Thurgau with "lighter, spicier cuisines, such as curry, Thai, Chinese, Cajun or Mexican." Duck Pond avers that its pinot gris is "excellent with shellfish, oysters, cheeses or cold chicken," and its gewürztraminer with "hors d'oeuvres, salads and white meats"; it has no reservations at all about its Clos d'Pond sweet white table wine, which, it suggests, you can "enjoy with any meal or alone."

■ SPECIALTIES OF THE HOUSE

In the past, most of the Wine Country's best dining rooms were in Portland and Eugene. But the culinary geography is changing, with superb restaurants springing up in smaller towns—Ashland, Dayton, Dundee, and even Roseburg. Now it's possible to have a world-class meal in rural districts that not so long ago were gastronomic backwaters. What follows is a short survey of some of the region's best restaurants, along with a few of their Oregon-accented specialties.

■ PORTLAND

In Portland, **Lucere** (1510 SW Harbor Way; 503-228-3233), on the Willamette, serves up Pacific Northwest dishes such as seared scallops with fennel, red onions, and oyster mushrooms; and duck with a blackberry sauce.

The **Heathman Hotel** has one of the state's best dining rooms (SW Broadway at Salmon Street; 503-241-4100). At breakfast, guests have feasted on crab cakes with crème fraîche and poached eggs; at lunch, on sautéed Oregon rockfish with an ancho chili–*beurre* fondue; at dinner, on ahi tuna wrapped in locally cured prosciutto and served with Oregon truffle risotto, on mushroom strudel with baby greens, and on roasted pesto salmon with a red onion–caper relish.

In downtown Portland, **Jo Bar & Rotisserie** (715 NW 23rd Avenue; 503-222-0048) has excelled with grilled and baked dishes—farmed steamer clams and crab sausage in a light fish stock, scented with red curry paste and baked in a

wood-burning oven; filet of salmon marinated in brown-rice vinegar, wrapped in mustard greens, and covered with sweet-potato "scales"; and whole rockfish studded with garlic and baked in an olive jus with a sea-salt skin. Jo Bar has also been celebrated for its wild-mushroom stew—chanterelles, porcinis, and shiitakes with pearl onions, baby carrots, and celery root, in a rich vegetable gravy.

Chef Vitaly Paley of **Paley's Place** (1204 NW 21st Avenue; 503-243-2403) has offered grilled radicchio and roasted organic beets with candied pecans, prosciutto, and parmesan crisps; and herbed pappardelle pasta with wild mushrooms, roasted squash, and truffle oil. His seafood dishes have included Pacific oysters with leeks, curry cream and apples over a cheddar biscuit; and pan-seared Alaskan king salmon with smoked bacon, red wine–braised onions, garnet yams, and apples. And he's done a splendid roasted rabbit with gruyère mashed potatoes, sautéed spinach, and mustard cream. Paley also has a clever "bacon and eggs" appetizer: a pan-fried duck egg served over a grilled brioche with smoky bacon, wild mushrooms, and a red-wine sauce.

Chef Cory Schreiber, who comes from an old Oregon family, made a splash a few years ago when he returned from California to open his own restaurant in northwest Portland, **Wildwood** (NW 21st Avenue and Overton Street; 503-248-9663). His salad of greens comes with fried oysters; pancetta is served with aioli on a chive crepe; and baked wild Oregon salmon arrives atop puréed sweet peas with marinated beets and spring onions in white balsamic vinegar. His fresh chanterelle pizza with herbs and cheese has been a local favorite; so have his skillet-roasted Washington mussels with garlic, tomato, saffron, and grilled bread; wood-roasted Washington chicken served on sweet-and-sour cabbage with brandied pears and grilled leeks; and red wine–braised duck legs.

■ WILLAMETTE VALLEY

But, as I said, excellent dining is no longer confined to Portland. Moving south from Portland, Ponzi Vineyards' **Dundee Bistro** (100A SW Seventh Street; 503-554-1650), right on Route 99W in the town of Dundee, serves excellent soups, salads, sandwiches, and pizzas, as well as an Oregon cheese platter with Sublimity cheese from Albany and other local artisanal cheeses.

Also in Dundee, **Red Hills Provincial Dining** (276 Highway 99W; 503-538-8224) serves an appetizer of fresh local figs with Oregon prosciutto, a salad Niçoise with fresh halibut and salmon instead of the traditional tuna, and Dungeness crab cakes with a sun-dried-tomato aioli.

In Dayton, the **Joel Palmer House** (600 Ferry Street; 503-864-2995) is *the* place to taste wild mushrooms; the recipe for one of its signature dishes—a wild-mushroom soup—has been in the owners' family for 50-plus years. Escargot served Willamette Valley style—with black chanterelles, garlic, and parsley—are delectable too. The standouts in McMinnville include **Nick's Italian Cafe** (521 NE Third Street; 503-434-4471), which serves steamed Manila clams and a rabbit braised in Oregon pinot gris and rosemary.

In Salem, **Kwan's Cuisine** (Mission and Commercial Streets; 503-362-7711) was the first restaurant to serve local salmon in a black-bean sauce, which goes surprisingly well with local pinot noir. Eugene's **Excelsior Cafe** (754 East 13th Avenue; 541-342-6963) has a boneless breast of chicken filled with a wonderful hazelnut-mascarpone mixture and topped with a pink-peppercorn champagne sauce, and grilled local lamb with a pinot noir sauce.

■ UMPQUA AND ROGUE RIVER VALLEYS

Two southerly restaurants have special salads. The small dining room at **La Garza Cellars** (491 Winery Lane; 541-679-9654), in the Umpqua Valley town of Roseburg, serves a Northwest salad with raisins, hazelnuts, and Oregon blue cheese. Ashland's **Monet Restaurant and Garden** (36 South Second Street; 541-482-1339), in the Rogue River Valley, serves shrimp steamed with white wine in a salad of organic greens, with a walnut-oil dressing.

■ ECLECTIC TASTES

And what wines do these distinguished restaurants recommend with their dishes? Pinot gris and pinot noir with salmon, of course. Merlot with lamb. Sémillon or sauvignon blanc with mollusks, Riesling with Dungeness crab. Some chefs love to pair local sparkling wine with salmon and pinot noir with oysters, rabbit, and scallops. But Oregon diners have eclectic tastes. Some insist on having white wine with meat and red wine with fish; others stick to the red or white of their choice through all the courses of a lengthy meal. Everybody's got a point of view, and the only rule left seems to be that there are no hard-and-fast rules.

Salads all in a row at the International Pinot Noir Celebration, to provide a change of pace for the palate.

■ NORTHWEST COOKERY AND OREGON WINES

Oregonians tend to be as unorthodox in cooking with wine as in pairing it with dishes. I've tasted an excellent lamb braised in a big, overblown chardonnay, oysters and mussels prepared with pinot noir, and salmon cooked in merlot. The characteristics of the wine—its flavor, its fruitiness, its acidity—and, of course, individual taste are far more important in Northwest cookery than a wine's color.

Helen Brown's West Coast Cook Book (1952), in discussing "the recipes of the pioneers of Oregon Territory . . . brought over the plains and changed to suit the supplies of the new land," points out that "many of these have a Yankee flavor"—a quality they often retain even in this more cosmopolitan era. The abundant bounty of the land and water have always inspired the state's cooks, and, according to James Beard, by the beginning of the 20th century, Oregon cooking had taken on an imaginative inventiveness. But it gradually slipped, along with the cooking in most of the country, and by the 1960s Oregon restaurants were seldom doing much better than a generic Continental style. Nonetheless, local cooking took a radical turn for the better in the 1970s and 1980s, when markets began stocking a much greater variety of fresh foods, and the availability of Oregon wines reinvigorated the scene further.

In her 1991 Northwest cookbook, *Dungeness Crabs and Blackberry Cobblers*, Janie Hibler, a Portland cooking-school teacher, talked about how impressive outsiders found the local bounty: "Professionals who came to teach were thrilled with the amazing selection of fresh seafood, fish, vegetables, and fruit. Once, a chef from La Varenne in Paris arrived for several classes. I had spent the morning racing all over town searching for the best and the freshest and was quite nervous as he rummaged through the boxes of food I had assembled. Finally he looked up and beamed. 'Ahhh, Portland is a little Paris. Just look at this beautiful food!'" I had the same experience when I took a New York magazine editor on a Portland grocery spree. Her eyes sparkled at the fresh local herbs, mushrooms, greens, beans, berries, and pears, and afterward she told me she would be hard pressed to match the freshness of these foods in New York City.

As local food and wine became the rage, Oregon cooks waxed exuberantly creative. Winery staffs led the vanguard by developing recipes that took full advantage of the wines they were producing. And so wineries handed out recipes for delectable dishes and recommended accompaniments: Henry Estate fillet of sole with spinach and Henry Estate chardonnay, and lamb chops in wine sauce with Henry Estate

Chef Cory Schreiber, of Portland's celebrated Wildwood, shows off his handiwork, a Dungeness crab and potato cake, with a salad of celery root and apple.

chardonnay (by Sylvia Henry); chardonnay salmon medallions Sokol Blosser and steak Sokol Blosser with pinot noir (by Bill Blosser and Susan Sokol Blosser); and Oregon mussels and clams with linguini and Tualatin Vineyards chardonnay (by Virginia Fuller, formerly of Tualatin Vineyards). Home cooks, inspired by the new creativity, came up with such delights as crawfish in cream sauce, served with Oregon chardonnay; and salmon caviar pie, with sauvignon blanc.

Cooks soon learned that Oregon wines, with their beautiful balance and a pleasantly high level of natural acids, lend themselves especially well to reduction sauces, bringing out the flavors of the foods cooked in them. Reduction enhances their high level of fruit, adding unexpected nuances to a dish; so does the varietal flavor of the grape, which tends to be more pronounced in the Northwest than in warmer growing regions. As a final benefit, they learned, the wine used in a dish doesn't just enhance and integrate its flavors; it also tenderizes meat and clams, especially when it's used in a marinade.

The region's cookery, like its wines, is still evolving. Still, its character is recognizable and distinctive. California, with its big, powerful wines and the hearty Mediterranean style of its cooking, is often likened to Provence or Tuscany. Oregon's new cuisine has a greater affinity with the more delicate preparations of northeastern and north-central France; if you're looking for a comparison, call it America's Alsace, or America's Burgundy. But the state's cooking has evolved so rapidly, and so radically, that there's no predicting what it might achieve over the next couple of decades.

Vast potential: pruned pinot noir grapevines in early spring.

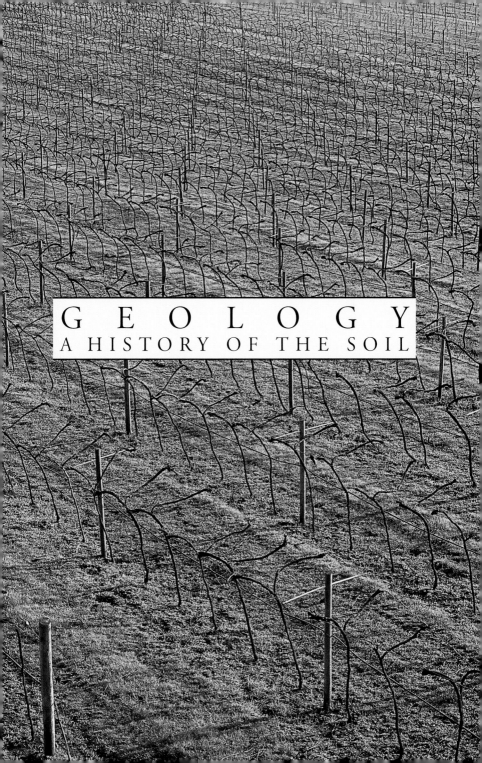

GEOLOGY
A HISTORY OF THE SOIL

■ FIRE, ICE, AND WATER

OREGON IS SYNONYMOUS WITH SPECTACULAR SCENERY: the rugged coastline, the steep-walled Columbia River Gorge with its towering waterfalls, the volcanic cones of Mount Hood and Mount Jefferson, the singular Crater Lake, the vast Oregon limestone caves. But the same geological forces that created these dramatic sites also created gentle hills and oak woods, meandering rivers and wildflower leas.

Many people think of western Oregon as a waterlogged region, and it's true that some of the best-known parts of the state become soggy in the winter. No vintner would think of planting vines in the really wet places—not because they wouldn't thrive, but because they wouldn't produce good wine. Other areas of western Oregon, though, have a Mediterranean climate, with warm, dry summers and temperate winters—the proper climate for growing grapes, as well as the proper soil. Grapes provide the most complex flavors when they're grown in well-drained soils and get little water; the vines, in other words, need to be stressed to give their best. Many parts of the Willamette, Umpqua, and Rogue River Valleys offer these basic growing conditions, but their great differences in geologic and climatic detail mean equally great differences in their wines.

What the three river valleys all have in common is the forces that created them: fire, ice, and water.

The fire came first. Some 15 million years ago, as oceanic and continental plates collided and pushed each other around, their friction brought about complex upliftings and foldings in the earth, turning ocean floors into mountaintops and plunging tall peaks into the sea. This friction created intense hot spots that melted down rocks into volcanic lava. Outflows of what is now known as Columbia Basin Basalt covered vast tracts east of the Cascades to a depth of as much as 5,000 feet; more lava flowed out through the Columbia River Gorge—all the way to the coast, where it can still be seen in the prominent capes it formed. It also flowed into the northern Willamette Valley, which until then had been a large bay of the Pacific Ocean, and left behind mountainous ridges, which over time eroded into low mountains and hills.

The top layer of these lava flows has transmogrified into a thick crust of red soils high in iron (which is what makes them red) and aluminum. Many of these soils, known technically as laterites, are in fact so bauxitic—that is, high in aluminum— that they would probably be mined instead of cultivated if their high iron content didn't make the process of extracting aluminum so much more expensive than

Majestic Mount Hood overlooks vineyards in the Chehalem Hills south of Portland.

extracting it from well-leached tropical bauxite soils. Laterite soils form in very moist, warm climates, and so the famed red soils of the Dundee, Eola, and South Salem Hills point to a wet and warm era in Oregon's distant past.

The ice and the water came after the fire. The lava crystallized into basalt during the final great ice age, which lasted, depending on the region, until between 15,000 and 12,000 years ago. Enormous ice lobes pushed south from Canada into what is now Washington State and flowed from the peaks of the Rockies and the Cascades down into the valleys. Little of this ice covered Oregon directly (except, perhaps, around the western Cascades), but western Oregon nevertheless felt its impact. It blocked the flow of the Columbia River in what is now northeastern and north-central Washington, diverting its waters south across the Columbia Plateau. It also blocked Montana's Clark's Fork River, near the modern-day city of Missoula, forming a vast lake known to geologists as Lake Missoula. The ice dam holding back the lake was unstable, and it broke, re-formed, and broke again and again over several millennia, each time sending a huge flood toward the sea. The last of these floods occurred about 12,000 years ago, at a time when human beings had already settled the region. (The giant floods are being commemorated at

Grapevines thrive in the loose, sandy loam that covers valleys and hillsides in western Oregon.

Spokane Floods National Park, which the U.S. government is in the process of establishing, with visitors centers in the Yakima and Willamette Valleys.)

As the floods roared across the land, they tore rock from the earth and ground it down into boulders, cobblestones, gravel, sand, and silt. The waters became turbid with debris. Wherever anything slowed or temporarily halted the floodwaters, this debris would settle as alluvial deposits. Most of eastern Washington's vineyards are planted on these deposits, which became the deep, quickly draining soils of the Yakima, Columbia, and Walla Walla Valleys. These soils are a mixture of ground granite from the mountains of British Columbia and Montana, pulverized Columbia Plateau basalt, and sedimentary and metamorphic rocks picked up en route. Their texture, meanwhile, ranges from fine silt clay to coarse sand and gravel. Because the floodwaters were deep, the alluvial deposits range far up the valleys; in places they even cover hills. At Canoe Ridge, in the Horse Heaven Hills of south-central Washington, they turned into loose, sandy loam scattered with chunks of basalt. Grapevines love these soils and quickly develop deep root systems to sustain themselves in times of drought.

No other part of the world has experienced such tremendous floods. The bed of the Columbia was too small to contain them, and the rushing waters spilled over the southern rim of its canyon in present-day northeastern Washington. They carved multiple channels—of which the Grand Coulee and Moses Coulee (between the Grand Coulee and the Columbia River) are the largest—on their course to the Wallula Gap, near the modern-day Tri-Cities (Pasco, Kennewick, and Richland) in southeastern Washington.

In some places the floods laid down extensive beds of gravels and even boulders. As the waters spilled into the Willamette Valley through a narrow gap in the Portland Hills, at present-day Oregon City, the waters slowed and deposited the heavier gravel, mostly around Portland and the northern Willamette Valley. The process continued as the floodwaters moved south, toward the head of the valley, laying the pattern that persists today: silt deposits grow increasingly finer as you move south, pockmarked by rocks that had been embedded in icebergs and floats. The slowed-down floodwaters formed a temporary lake that was, at about 350 feet, deep enough to submerge lower mountain slopes and hills. It didn't quite reach all the way to the present-day city of Eugene, which sits at an elevation of about 400 feet. This is one reason the soils of the southern Willamette Valley (and the resulting wines) are so different from those of the north.

Children in a Southern Willamette Valley vineyard, ca. 1900

Some Willamette Valley vineyards are planted on these sediments. Others grow on the ancient laterite soils mentioned above, which predate not only the floods but the valley itself, as well as the Coast Range and the Cascade Mountains on either side. Many are planted on a mixture: the floods intermingled their debris with the already existing laterite soils, making for the complicated patchwork of soils in the region today. That's a big reason that Oregon Wine Country soils (and the wines they produce) differ so markedly from one vineyard to the next.

The Willamette Valley splits into two smaller valleys: the Northern Basin, which stretches from the Oregon City Gap (where the Willamette River breaks through the mountains on its way to join the Columbia) to Salem; and the Southern Basin, north of Eugene, which is also the flattest part of the valley. Between the two basins rise the Eola Hills, the South Salem Hills, and several other humps jutting up from the valley floor. At the northern end of the Northern Basin are the Tualatin Mountains, the Red Hills of Dundee, and the Chehalem Mountains (all prime wine regions); the southern end of the Southern Basin is pinched off near Eugene, where the Coast Range pushes up against the Western Cascade Mountains.

A curious natural feature of the Willamette Valley is the numerous isolated hills, known locally as buttes, that dot it. Rising to a height of several hundred feet, they are volcanic in origin and predate the valley itself; geologists suspect they rose up at a time when the valley was still a bay of the Pacific. Their steep slopes have many of the same vine-friendly soils as the rest of the valley, but few of them have yet been planted to vineyards; they're too steep for easy cultivation.

The Umpqua and Rogue River Valleys farther south grew out of cataclysms of their own. The geologically complex Hundred Valleys of the Umpqua formed when the Coast Range slammed into the Klamath Mountains. The mineral-rich Klamaths are a sort of three-dimensional mosaic formed from bits and pieces of islands and subcontinents that came to a temporary rest in southern Oregon and northern California. The Oregon side is drained by the Rogue River and its tributaries, the Applegate and the Illinois. Bear Creek, which flows through modern-day Medford, marks the boundary between the Klamath Mountains and the western Cascades. Vineyards here are planted on a variety of porous soils that were weathered from the rocks of the nearby mountains and then deposited by rivers and streams on or near the valley floor.

■ MOUNTAINS, CLIMATE, AND VEGETATION

But more than the soils determines the quality of Oregon wines. High mountains exert a tremendous effect on the climate. The Coast Range blocks sea air from the Willamette Valley, fostering cool winters and warm, dry summers. These westerly mountains came into being when the North American continent, on its relentless westward march, scraped over the oceanic Farallon Plate, tearing off accumulated sediments and odd pieces of volcanic rock, which eventually rose to mountain height. Coast Range peaks have an average height of 1,500 feet, with a few topping 3,000 feet; Mary's Peak, southwest of Corvallis, is the highest, at 4,097 feet. They aren't quite high enough to fully block the seasonal rains coming in from the Pacific, and so the Willamette Valley is a lot wetter (in winter) than the Columbia and Walla Walla wine valleys east of the Cascades. Still, the Coast Range protects the Willamette Valley from the ocean well enough to raise growing-season temperatures, creating conditions just right for the ripening of the difficult pinot noir grape.

The soils that nourish Oregon grapes are also good to flowers at the Rogue River Valley's Foris Vineyards. (following pages) Verdant vines at Montinore Vineyards in Washington County.

APPELLATIONS

Is wine made in the vineyard or in the winery? French winemakers, who believe in the importance of the *terroir* (the soil, the microclimate, the growing conditions), would argue the former. Oregon winemakers—not all of whom grow their own grapes—have generally claimed the latter, though this is changing as they get to know the land and learn which grapes do best in a certain location. But Oregonians have always recognized that growing areas play a role in the quality of grapes. When a specific region has unique soil, climate, and other growing conditions, wineries located within it can petition the Acohol Tobacco Tax and Trade Bureau to designate it as an American Viticultural Area (AVA), more commonly called an appellation. (Until recently, this was the job of the Bureau of Alcohol, Tobacco, and Firearms.) Different appellations are renowned for different wines, and it is common to find an appellation mentioned on a label. In Oregon, this can be done only if 90 percent of the grapes used to make the wine were grown in that appellation. Oregon winemakers have also begun to acknowledge that grapes grown in particular vineyards differ widely in quality, and the best vineyards also are frequently mentioned on wine labels. More AVAs are expected to be approved in the coming years, but as of this writing, the state had a half dozen.

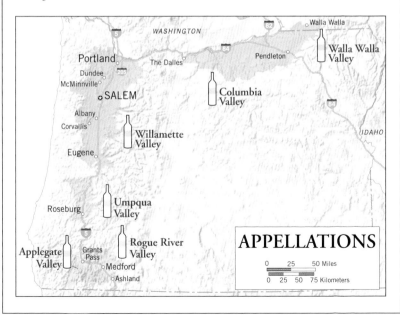

Sea air flowing up the Siuslaw River helps cool some southern Willamette Valley vineyards. Properly speaking, these vineyards aren't in the Willamette Valley itself but in the foothills of the Coast Range, on slopes above the Siuslaw and its tributaries. The Siuslaw doesn't cut all the way through the Coast Range, as the Umpqua and Rogue do to the south, but stops short at Green Ridge, a few miles southwest of Cottage Grove, bringing the flow of cool marine air to a halt—which makes the valley of the Willamette River's Coast Fork east of the ridge much hotter than the valleys to the west, one reason the latter have vineyards and the former do not.

The soils here are as well drained as those of the Willamette Valley proper, but in content they're different, having developed from marine deposits that were lifted when tectonic forces pushed the Coast Range up out of the earth. Many of the volcanic outcroppings that dot the region erupted beneath hundreds (possibly thousands) of feet of seawater eons ago, when this region was ocean floor. Like the Siuslaw, the Umpqua River, which cuts through the Coast Range nearly at sea level, allows cooling marine breezes to flow far inland. Not so the turbulent, twisted Rogue River, whose sheltered valleys constitute the Pacific Northwest's warmest growing region, where an almost Californian climate encourages Mediterranean grapes to thrive.

Although many characteristics of Oregon Wine Country soils were determined in the very distant past, others were formed more recently—by rain, sun, wind, frost, and other forces of nature. Vegetation plays a role, as it decomposes into the soil, and also serves as an indicator of the soils it covers (and of local microclimates), since different soils attract different plants and form different ecological communities. In western Oregon, you can often tell the nature of the local soil by looking at the native vegetation. Is it covered with oaks or with pines? Chaparral or Douglas fir? Grasses or ash trees? There seems to be an affinity between grapevines and both oaks and pines—which may go back to the vines' ancient Mediterranean home—but grapes growing on land once occupied by maples and Douglas firs also make good wine. Only time will tell whether the vines themselves modify their soil and, ultimately, the quality of the wine.

The different soils of the Willamette Valley interlock like a complicated jigsaw puzzle. But a few main soils predominate. In recent years, vintners have argued as to whether Willakenzie or Jory soils produce better wines, and have even held comparative tastings of pinot noir grown on the different soils. (The jury's still out.)

Willakenzie soils, dark brown and moderately deep, derive from sandstone and tuffaceous materials. Dark reddish-brown Jory soils (the Red Hills of Dundee are named for their predominantly Jory soils) have mostly been weathered from basic igneous bedrock. Jory soils are moderately acidic, Willakenzie soils slightly to moderately acidic—which is unusual for wine-friendly soils, because grapevines seem to prefer neutral to somewhat alkaline soils.

Both Willakenzie and Jory soils drain exceptionally well, and the early pioneer settlers apparently recognized the agricultural promise of them, because they cleared most of the native oaks and firs off them and planted them with orchards. Today, these lands are increasingly being planted with grapevines. The Eola Hills, northwest of Salem, have Nekia soils, derived from weathered basalt and tuffaceous rocks—dark reddish-brown, well-drained, moderately acid, and, like Willakenzie and Jory soils, perfect for cultivating grapes.

But these soils are only the beginning. Vines are flexible, and they thrive in many different soils and as many different microclimates. Analyzing these differences will remain a major part of enological studies for decades to come. Some even wonder whether Oregon's best vineyard soils have been discovered yet. Robert Louis Stevenson gave voice to a similar question well over a century ago, when he lived for a short time in California's Napa Valley. In *The Silverado Squatters,* he wrote of the area's fledgling wine industry:

> The beginning of vine-planting is like the beginning of mining for
> the precious metals: the wine-grower also "Prospects" . . . . Those
> lodes and pockets of earth, more precious than the precious ores, that
> yield inimitable fragrance of soft fire; whose virtuous Bonanza, where
> the soil has sublimated under the sun and stars to something finer,
> and the wine is bottled poetry; these still lie undiscovered; chaparral
> conceals, thicket embowers them . . . . But there they bide their hour,
> awaiting their Columbus; and nature nurses and prepares them.

Stevenson may have been wrong in believing that those soils still lay hidden, and contemporary skeptics may also be off the mark. The finest soils may in fact be in plain view, in today's vineyards—but it may take hundreds of years of cultivation to coax out their poetry. Vineyards, like the finest wines, may simply need more time to properly mature. But then, what are a few hundred years in the search for great wines?

The fine art of tasting begins with swirling wine in the glass.

VISITING WINERIES
TASTING AND TOURING

The splendid winery grounds at Bridgeview, in the Illinois River Valley.

OREGON'S VINEYARDS SPRAWL over steep hillsides and gentle slopes, perching amid windswept mountaintops and nestling in lush creek valleys. Few of the world's other wine regions have a greater variety of geographical marvels, or more beautiful wineries. Some of these wineries have charmingly tended gardens, like the ones at Rex Hill, Duck Pond, Argyle, and Henry Estate. Bridgeview even has a swan pond. Some take advantage of a superb natural setting, as do Foris, Amity, Chateau Benoit, Ponzi, and Sokol Blosser (with its views, on a clear day, of distant Mount Jefferson).

There's nothing more enchanting than perching yourself high up on a gentle south-facing slope and gazing down upon verdant fields and pastures, with only the occasional woodlot or orchard to break up the long rows of grape-laden vines marching down the hill. Behind you, shaded by Douglas firs, big-leaf maples, and oaks, stands a rustic, weathered building—the winery you've come to visit. Birds trill as you unload the ice chest in which you've packed your lunch, setting it on one of the vine-shaded picnic tables. And then you head for the tasting room, to sample some wines and select a special bottle to accompany your meal.

■ IN THE TASTING ROOM

The tasting room is usually well marked; it's generally a winery's most visitor-friendly feature. Don't worry if you know nothing about wine. Tasting rooms are very relaxed places, designed to introduce novices to the pleasures of wine and give enophiles a chance to expand their knowledge. If you're a novice, everyone will be glad to help (though some wineries hire inexperienced workers, at minimum or near-minimum wage, who know little about even the wines they're pouring). There's no magic to tasting; all you need is a palate and common sense. You evaluate wine by appearance, aroma, and flavor.

■ APPEARANCE

No matter whether it's a white, a red, or a rosé, a wine should be clear, without cloudiness or sediment. Hold the glass up to a window so that natural light can flow through the liquid and show up any cloudiness. Next, the color: is it right for the wine? A white should be golden—straw, medium, or deep, depending on the type. The deepest gold is appropriate in a rich, sweet dessert wine but out of place in a chardonnay or a sauvignon blanc. A rosé should be a clear pink—not too red, and without touches of orange or brown. Usually a brown tinge in a white or a rosé indicates that it's over the hill or that it's been stored badly. Reds may have a violet tinge when young, an amber one when well aged. At that stage it's permissible, too, for reds to have sediment, but the wine should be decanted into a serving vessel—the glass isn't the proper place to let these deposits settle. A definite brown color is a flaw in reds. So is paleness, unless you're looking at a pinot noir; the wine made from this grape can be extremely pale.

■ AROMA

After you've looked the wine over, swirl it gently and stick your nose into the glass. While a wine's appearance—its color and clarity—may give you a good initial clue as to its potential, its aroma may be its most important attribute. Some wines have simple aromas; others have multiple, nuanced aromas. To release the aroma, gently swirl the wine in your glass in order to let it mix with a little air; this will tell you a lot about the wine before you take your first sip.

A wine doesn't have to be complex to be enjoyable. But its aroma should be clean and pleasing. It should never be off; it should never smell of sauerkraut, wet cardboard, garlic, wet dog, or skunk—all odors listed on the official Wine Aroma

Wheel of the American Society for Enology and Viticulture, along with moldy, horsey, mousy, and sweaty. Nor should your glass smell of broccoli, bell peppers, or other vegetables—all signs that the wine is badly made. And it should never give a hint of vinegar, a sure sign of spoilage. You'll also want to sniff for such chemical faults as sulfur or too much wood vanillin from oak.

Fortunately, most aromas in a wine are more appealing. Grapes are a complex fruit, and their fermented juice can evoke all sorts of different scents, often at the same time. Look for apricots, peaches, ripe melon, honey, and wildflowers in white wines; black pepper, cherry, violets, and cedar in reds. Rosés are made from red grapes, so they have aromas similar to those of reds but on a more gentle plane—plus raspberry, geranium, and perhaps a touch of pomegranate. Each varietal, or type of grape, has its own distinct aroma—which, with experience, you'll learn to recognize. Wine with good varietal character is better than wine with an indistinct aroma.

■ FLAVOR

After you finish the looking, swirling, and sniffing, you're ready to take your first sip. You'll note that, in addition to flavor, the wine has texture (often described as mouth feel), ranging from light to thick ("full-bodied"). Swirl the wine around in your mouth. Does it feel pleasant? Does it seem to fill your mouth, or is it thin and weak?

Now, the flavor. The human palate can process only four tastes: sweet, sour, salty, and bitter—and salt is not a natural component of wine. If you've discovered some light bitterness in a young red, taste again; you'll discover that the wine's tannic tartness can fool the palate. True bitterness—acrid, unpleasant bitterness—is a fault, but it's rare in wine. Sweetness is a component of many wines, even some that make claims to being dry. Many Northwest wines, even table wines like chardonnay and cabernet sauvignon, have become sweeter in recent years, probably because of the American consumer's sweet tooth. But it's a very light sweetness, barely at the threshold of perception. When you taste a wine, you'll notice more than just the four basic flavors, of course. That's because your nose plays a bigger role in tasting than your palate does. A taster swirls wine in the mouth, or "chews" it, not only to text the texture but also for the same reason as swirling it in the glass: to release the aromas. The more aromas a wine has, and the more complex their interaction, the more interesting it is.

2 0 0 1

Vintage: At least 95 percent of the grapes used to make the wine were harvested in 2001.

Winery name

WILLAKENZIE ESTATE

Croft

OREGON

Pinot Noir

WILLAMETTE VALLEY

PRODUCED & BOTTLED BY

WILLAKENZIE ESTATE, YAMHILL, OREGON

ALC. 13.9 BY VOL.

Vineyard name: The grapes were grown at the Croft Vineyard, a portion of which the winery leases.

Varietal composition: At least 90 percent of the grapes in this wine are pinot noir.

Appellation: All the grapes were grown in the Willamette Valley American Viticultural Area.

Production: The wine was produced and bottled by the winery itself, not a third party (though WillaKenzie purchased the grapes from another grower).

ADDITIONAL LABEL TERMS

Estate grown: The grapes came from vineyards the winery owns or operates.

Estate bottled: The grapes were estate grown, and the wine was bottled at the winery, with both winery and vineyard in same appellation.

Reserve: An inexact term that means "special," this can refer to something special about how or where the grapes were grown or how the wine was made.

TRUTH IN LABELING

Oregon has the nation's strictest labeling regulations. All the grapes used to produce a wine must come from the area indicated on the label—the Willamette Valley, for example, or the Rogue River Valley. Varietal wines must contain at least 90 percent of the grape variety named on the label—the national standard is 75 percent—with the exception of cabernet sauvignon, which may contain up to 25 percent of traditional Bordeaux blending grapes— cabernet franc, merlot, malbec, petit verdot. Finally, 95 percent of the wine in the bottle must come from the vintage year stated on the label.

Glasses wined up and ready for a tasting.

Next, it's time to evaluate the acidity. All wine has acid; it's necessary to balance the fruit of the wine and give it stability. But it should be an acidity you taste but don't smell. If a wine smells acidic, it has started turning into vinegar. Northwest wines have an advantage over other wines because their acidity occurs naturally. In hotter regions, winemakers sometimes add acid to their wine (by sprinkling in acid crystals) to give it stability—to hold it together during fermentation and aging. Oregon's growing season is ideal: long warm (even hot) summer days, which load the grapes with fruitiness and sugar, and short cool nights, which preserve acids.

At the same time, taste the wine for sugar. A dinner wine should have no perceptible sweetness; a dessert wine commonly has quite a bit. Swallow. Do you like the flavor? Does it relate to the aroma? If not, something's out of balance. Does it go down nicely, or does your throat feel like it's puckering up?

Most important, you should ask yourself if you *like* the wine. If you don't, then don't drink any more. Though you may learn to appreciate a wine you don't understand, a wine will never really appeal to you unless you like it. A wine can be technically perfect, but the parts are less important than the whole, and the whole may bore you. Remember: you're the one who decides. It's your taste that matters.

■ TASTING ROOM TIPS

There are several other things to keep in mind in the tasting room. Don't overdo it—*especially* if you're driving. Those little sips add up. And don't feel like you have to buy a bottle just because the winery has given you a taste or two. No one expects you to. Tasting rooms are there to familiarize potential customers with a winery's products. What the winery hopes is that you'll like the wine enough to buy it at your wine shop or supermarket. The things to stock up on at wineries are hard-to-find vintages and varietals—the wines you can't get at home. Sometimes these can be bought only at the winery. If you're from outside the region, ask about the winery's direct-shipment program. Most wineries now ship wine directly to consumers, but only to those in states that allow reciprocal shipments.

There's another good reason for buying Northwest wines right from the winery and coddling the bottles all the way home: some Northwest wines do not ship well. Moreover, even those that do may suffer from improper storage at the distributor's, or at a grocery store's warehouse. Unfortunately—and I write from sad experience—many of the wines for sale even at Northwest grocery stores and wine shops have gone bad on the shelves. It's maddening to open an expensive bottle of wine only to learn that it has spoiled before you could take your first sip.

GRAPE VARIETIES

■ WHITE

CHARDONNAY

This noble white Burgundian varietal has been made into good wine in Oregon, though it has struggled during most vintages. Oregon growers claim that the wrong clones were planted and hope that new plantings of different clones will improve quality.

PINOT BLANC

When grown in well-drained soils of Oregon's cool vineyards, this white grape can create a wine that rivals chardonnay.

PINOT GRIS

This white grape does well almost anywhere in the state, even in the warm southern valleys of the Umpqua and Rogue Rivers. It makes more interesting wine in Oregon than chardonnay.

RIESLING

Also called white Riesling, this cool-climate grape has been upstaged in many vineyards by chardonnay, but when the conditions are right it makes good wine in Oregon.

VIOGNIER

This white grape from France's Rhône Valley makes distinguished wines with fruity bouquets in Oregon, especially in the warm southern valleys.

■ RED

CABERNET FRANC

Cabernet franc can produce aromatic red wines, softer and subtler than those of the closely related cabernet sauvignon, especially when planted in warmer vineyards of the Umpqua or Rogue regions.

CABERNET SAUVIGNON

This noble red grape of Bordeaux has struggled in Oregon's cool northern vineyards but is coming into its own in the state's warm southern vineyards.

MERLOT

The wines produced in the Umpqua and Rogue River Valleys by this dark, blue-black grape are often excellent, soft yet complex even when young.

PINOT NOIR

Great wines have been made from this finicky grape in the cool growing regions of the Willamette Valley.

SANGIOVESE

This versatile Tuscan grape grows well in the Umpqua River and Rogue River Valleys, where it produces light-bodied yet long-lived, very complex reds.

ZINFANDEL

In some of southern Oregon's warmer vineyards this grape produces complex, well-balanced wines.

(top) Young pinot blanc vines grow in protective tubes. (bottom) Close-up of pinot noir.

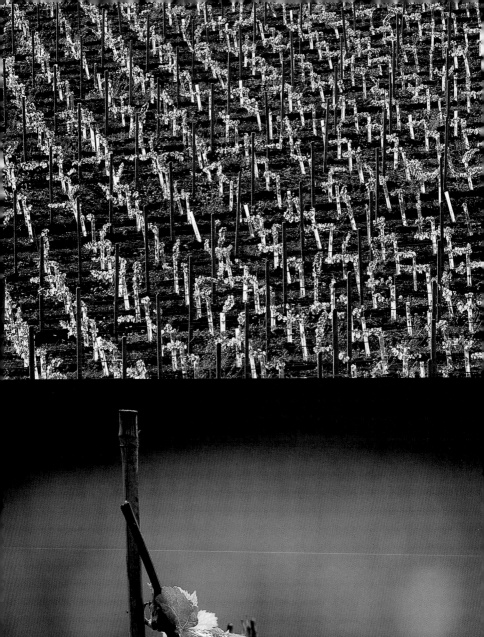

■ THE WINE-MAKING PROCESS

In addition to tasting, you should consider touring a winery or two to see how wine is made. Winery tours are particularly informative between August and October, when most of the grapes ripen and are crushed and fermented. At other times of the year, winery work consists of monitoring the wine, racking it (that is, transferring it from one tank or barrel to another in order to leave deposits behind), and bottling and boxing finished wine.

In today's complicated wine market—with more wineries and fewer distributors to handle their wines—visiting the Wine Country is about the only way to find out about what's happening and to discover the obscure winery producing that elusive, extraordinary wine you've always dreamed of tasting. A winery tour has a further value: it provides proof that a winery actually makes the wine it sells. During the past decade, custom-crushing has become increasingly popular, especially with smaller wineries that can't afford the large capital outlay that production and storage facilities require. In the most benign version of this practice, a small winery delivers its grapes to a larger one, which crushes them and drains the must into tanks, which are then returned to the original winery to be fermented, aged, and bottled. In the worst version, winery owners go to a custom-crush facility, specify what sort of grapes they want to buy (and how much they want to spend for them), and then have the custom facility harvest the grapes; crush, ferment, age, and bottle them; and deliver the wine to them completely finished—or even sell it for them. It amounts to owning a winery without having to get your fingers dirty. One way that you, as a consumer, can protect yourself against such practices is by carefully studying the label, whose text has to meet legal standards. Does it say, "Grown, produced, and bottled by Yadda Yadda Winery"? Or does it say, "Produced and bottled by . . . ," or merely "Bottled for . . ."? *Caveat emptor.*

I don't mean to imply that custom-crushed wine is necessarily bad. Some of it has even won (and deserved) prestigious awards. But an enophile wants to know the truth—and sleuthing adds an enthralling angle to winery tours.

Wineries differ, of course, and so do their methods. Most Northwest wineries store their wines in warehouses, but a few of them have caves (pronounced "kahvz," from the French)—long tunnels bored into hillsides, where wine stays naturally at an even temperature. Sparkling wine isn't made the same way chardonnay and pinot noir are, and large wineries and small wineries operate differently.

HOW FINE WINE IS MADE

Stemmer-Crusher: Removes the grapes from their stems and crushes their skins so juice can flow off freely.

Juice that flows from crushed grapes before pressing is called "free-run."

Wine Press: An inflatable bag that gently pushes the grape pulp against a perforated drum.

Fermentation: The process by which the natural fruit sugars of grapes are converted, with the aid of yeasts, into alcohol. Takes place in large vats or tanks or small oak barrels.

White wines are not fermented with pulp and skins. The grapes are pressed before fermentation.
White wines may be fermented in small barrels. They are often cool-fermented to preserve their fruitiness.

Racking: After fermentation, wine is racked, that is, moved to new, clean barrels, to aid clarification.
It may be filtered or fined or allowed to settle naturally.

Aging: Many premium wines are aged in small oak barrels. Keeping wine in oak too long, though, kills delicate grape flavors and may make the wine taste "woody."

Red wines are fermented with pulp and skins. Some grapes are pressed after fermentation.

Bottling: After wine has been clarified it is ready for bottling.
Very small wineries still bottle by hand, but most bottling is done by machine in the sterile environment of a special enclosure, to keep impurities out of the bottle.

Below I've sketched the general process by which wine is made, but you'll find variations at every winery. The best way to learn about winemaking is to visit different types of wineries and compare their methods.

One final note: always remember to double-check a winery's opening hours, either by phone or on its Web site, before you visit. Winery hours vary wildly—and wineries have an annoying habit of changing their hours. You'll save yourself considerable frustration if you take a moment to check before you make the trip out.

Pinot noir grapes are poured into the stemmer-crusher at Van Duzer Vineyards, west of Salem. (following spread) Picking grapes at Tyee Wine Cellars, near Corvallis in the Southern Willamette Valley (top left) and at Yamhill Valley Vineyards in Yamhill County (bottom left). After harvesting, grapes are delivered to the crush pad at Yamhill (right).

■ AFTER THE HARVEST

At some wineries, grapes are harvested by machines; at others, they're still picked by hand—it depends on the terrain and the type of grape. White-wine grapes are sometimes picked at night—powerful floodlights illuminate the fields—especially delicate white varietals like chardonnay. The grapes contain natural fruit acids, which not only bring out the fruit flavors in the finished wine but also give the wine its backbone. Grape acids decrease during the day, when the sun heats the grapes, and increase during the cool hours of the night; picking white-wine grapes at night yields the best acid. Red-wine grapes are a different matter, because they get so much of their acids from their skins.

Workers haul in the grapes in large containers called gondolas. At the crush pad (where winery tours generally start), they unload the bunches onto a conveyor belt, handling them carefully so that none of their juice is lost. The conveyor belt drops the grape clusters into a stemmer-crusher, a machine with a drum equipped with steel fingers designed to knock the grapes off the stems and crush their skins so that their juice can flow off freely. The grapes and the juice fall through a grate, and stainless-steel pipes carry them to a press or vat. The stems and leaves are recycled in the vineyards as a natural fertilizer.

■ PRESSING AND FERMENTATION

What happens at the next stage depends on the type of grape and the type of wine it's destined for—white, red, or rosé.

The juice of **white-wine grapes** goes to settling tanks, where the skins and other solids separate from the clear free-run juice and settle to the bottom. The juice is pumped directly to a fermenter, either a stainless-steel tank (which may be insulated to keep the fermenting juice cool) or an oak barrel. The skins and other solids on the bottom of the settling tank still contain a lot of juice, so they're dropped into a press. Modern presses have a perforated drum with a Teflon-coated bag inside, which inflates like a balloon, pushing the grapes, slowly and gently, against the drum's wall; the liquids squeezed from the solids flow off through the perforations.

Press juice and free-run juice are fermented separately. A little press juice may be added to the free-run juice, to heighten complexity—but not too much, because press juice tends to be too strongly flavored, and some of the flavors may not be desirable. Press juice is fermented in stainless-steel tanks. Free-run juice may be handled differently. In the case of chardonnay and some sauvignon blanc, it's fermented

in small oak barrels, in individual batches, separated and labeled by vineyard and lot. At least, that's how the very best white wines are made—and it's why they're so expensive. The process is labor intensive, and the oak barrels, imported from France, are costly and can be used for only a few years. (Although French oak is the wood traditionally used for aging wine, many wineries are starting to experiment with Oregon oak.)

Barrel-aging rooms are kept dark, because both light and the heat that lights generate can damage the fermenting wine. Sauvignon blanc and Riesling are commonly fermented in stainless-steel tanks, which may be equipped with wraparound cooling sleeves to encourage fruit aromas and delicacy. Chardonnay, like some red wines, may be, as noted, fermented in small oak barrels, a process that creates depth and complexity as the wine picks up vanilla and other harmonious flavors from the wood. When the wine is finished, several batches are carefully blended together—a step that gives the winemaker a further chance to perfect the wine.

Red-wine grapes are crushed like white-wine grapes, but the juice isn't separated from the skins and pulp during fermentation, because they give the wine its color. After crushing, both the juice and the solids are pumped into vats and fermented together. The must is left on the skins for varying periods of time, depending on how much color the winemaker wants to extract.

Reds are more robust than whites because fermentation extracts not only color but also flavors and tannins (special acids that help the wine age) from the skins. The fermentation is carried out at warmer temperatures than it is for whites— about 70 to 90 degrees Fahrenheit (from 21 to 32 degrees Centigrade), as opposed to from 50 to 59 degrees Fahrenheit (from 10 to 15 degrees Centigrade) for whites. As the grape sugars turn into alcohol, they generate large amounts of carbon dioxide, which is lighter than the wine but heavier than the air above it, and so forms a cover that protects the wine from oxidation.

As the red wine ferments, the skins rise to the top, and have to be mixed back in periodically (so that the wine can extract the maximum amount of color and flavor). The winemaker either punches them down manually (the traditional way) or pumps the wine from the bottom of the fermenter back to the top, to break up the "cap" of spent grape skins. Punching down—the method practiced in traditional

(opposite) A worker at Valley View Vineyards pours harvested grapes into a gondola.
(following spread) Wines aging in oak barrels at Lange Winery in Yamhill County. Oak contains natural tannins, which the wine extracts from the barrels.

European wineries—is preferable, because it keeps the carbon dioxide cover intact and minimizes the wine's exposure to oxygen. (The fumes, incidentally, make working with wine at this stage potentially dangerous. In November 2002, a British Columbia winery owner, overcome by fumes, fell into a 600-gallon fermentation tank and drowned; his winemaker died while trying to rescue him.)

At the end of fermentation, the free-run wine is drained off; the skins and pulp go to a press, which extracts the remaining wine. As with whites, the winemaker may choose to add a little of the press wine to the free-run wine for the sake of complexity. Otherwise the press juice goes into bulk wine.

Bottles ready for shipment from the Southern Willamette Valley's Silvan Ridge/Hinman Vineyards.

Rosé or blush wines are also made from red-wine grapes, but in their case the must is left on the skins for hours instead of days. When the juice has reached the desired color, it's drained off and filtered; yeast is added, and the wine is fermented like any other. Because rosé stays on the skins for a shorter time, it also attracts fewer tannins, making it lighter than red wine. Thus rosé is really a lighter, fruitier red wine—not a pink version of white wine.

■ RACKING, FINING, AND AGING

When the wine has finished fermenting, either in tanks or in barrels, it is *racked*— that is, moved into clean tanks or barrels to separate it from the lees, the spent yeast and any grape solids that have dropped out of the liquid. At this stage, the winemaker may (or may not) decide to filter the wine or to clarify it in a centrifuge. Chardonnay and some special batches of sauvignon blanc may be "left on the lees" (allowed to stay in contact with them) for extended periods to pick up extra complexity.

If the wine has been aged for a significant length of time, it will be racked again, and it may also be *fined*—that is, clarified with the addition of such fining agents as bentonite (a powdery clay) or albumen (egg white), both of which draw off impurities. Some winemakers filter their wines, especially white wines; others only fine them. Wine may be filtered after fermentation, before bottling, or whenever the winemaker thinks it necessary. After white wine is bottled, it isn't kept in storage for long. Most of it goes to a cooperative warehouse, which ships it on demand. At many wineries, only the reserve wines—their most special wines—are aged in the wineries' own cellars.

After red wine has been racked, it ages in oak barrels for a year or longer. Unlike the barrels used for aging chardonnay, those used for aging reds aren't always new. They may have already been used for chardonnay, which has extracted most of their flavors. Oak, like grapes, contains natural tannins, and the wine extracts these tannins from the barrels. Oak also has countless tiny pores, through which the water in the wine slowly evaporates, making the wine more concentrated. This evaporation creates more exposed surface, so to prevent the aging wine from oxidizing, the barrels must be regularly topped off with wine from the same vintage—another reason that aged wine is more expensive. Some reds are left unfined for extra depth.

■ TASTE TEST

The only way even the best winemaker can tell that a wine is finished is by tasting it. A winemaker constantly tastes wines as they ferment, as they age in tanks or barrels, and—regularly, though less often—as they age in bottles. Is the wine ready to be moved from fermenters into vats or barrels? Does it need to be fined or racked? Is its color right? Can it stand on its own merits, or should it be blended with other wines from the same vintage? If it's a cabernet or merlot, would it benefit by having another red blended in, to soften it or to make it more complex? If it's a sauvignon blanc, would it benefit from the addition of, say, sémillon? And so forth. The winemaker rarely dares take a vacation until the wines are finished, and the wine is released (winemaker jargon for sent to market) only when the winemaker's palate and nose say it's ready.

Because Oregon's wineries are small and the state's winemakers prefer to vinify grapes from different vineyards separately, everything is done on a small scale. You seldom, for example, see the giant stainless-steel vats so commonly used for aging in California and some Washington wineries. This small scale allows for an attention to detail that enormous operations can't begin to rival—and that's a significant plus for the consumer.

Row upon row of grapevines at the David Hill Winery.

WASHINGTON COUNTY

STANDING IN DOWNTOWN PORTLAND on a clear day, you can see not only the white snowcap of Mount Hood to the east but also a fringe of green hills that holds the promise of countryside beyond the bridges and office towers of the city. These forested hills seem most pristine to the west—but their appearance is misleading, for on the other side of that green ridge, in the formerly very rural Washington County, suburbia has arrived. This county, which spreads across the Tualatin Mountains and Tualatin Plains from the outskirts of Portland west to the Coast Range, has a dual personality.

Washington County is the most urbanized of Oregon's wine counties. Its eastern part, in the western suburbs of Portland, is often called Silicon Forest for its concentration of technology companies, among them Intel, Tektronix, and NEC. The athletic-wear maker Nike also has its world headquarters here. The young,

(preceding pages) Snowy Mount Hood stands watch over Tualatin Valley vineyards.
(above) The Forest Grove vineyards, established in 1883, now the home of David Hill Winery.

affluent, educated population that these companies have attracted provides the perfect market for locally produced wines.

Some of the county's former farming towns, including Beaverton, Hillsboro, Tigard, Tualatin, and Forest Grove, have long clustered into metropolitan Portland. But the remaining open spaces more than make up for the dreary stretches of housing tracts and shopping malls. So far, Washington County has managed to preserve more than 75 percent of its agricultural and forest lands. Miles of rivers, trails, and bike paths wind through its grape-growing areas. And because the suburbs sprang up so recently, the local wildlife hasn't yet fully dispersed. Don't be surprised to see beavers, ducks, marsh wrens, and red-winged blackbirds on a pond behind a Beaverton motel. With luck, you might even spot a bald eagle.

These hills and valleys were among the first in Oregon to attract white settlers, back in the mid-1800s, because the open prairies offered the prospect of planting crops without first having to perform the backbreaking task of logging primeval forests and grubbing out tree stumps. In 1834, the Hudson's Bay Company's chief factor (or trader), John Work, wrote this about the region when he traveled south from Fort Vancouver:

> The soil is composed of a thick strata of dark vegetable mould perhaps not over 6 or 8 inches deep, over a bed of reddish tile. No stone or gravel worth mentioning. It is not thickly wooded with timber but overgrown with underwood. . . . On reaching the plains some oak of a middling size fringe the edges of the woods. . . . The country on geting out of the woods has a beautiful appearance. It is a continuation of plains which commence here and continue on to the Southward. . . .

A more modern, more thorough analysis reveals that the soils consist of deep silt deposits, more than a thousand feet thick in some places, intermingled with pebbles. The giant Spokane floods inundated the valleys during the last ice age, lapping up against the mountains and leaving behind deep layers of pebbles, gravel, and silt. That these alluvial soils are so young, in geologic terms, is what makes them so perfect for growing grapes: all those pebbles and the porous, gritty soils provide superb drainage. Many of the soils higher up on the slopes, out of reach of the floodwaters, are laterites similar in structure and mineral content (they are very high in aluminum) to the red soils of the Dundee Hills to the south; equally well drained, they're also excellent for growing grapes.

Wheat was this region's first cash crop. In the horse-and-wagon age, the Tualatin Plains and the hills bordering the Tualatin River Valley were within easy reach of Portland's burgeoning population and its port. But vineyards were also established here quite early, and several contemporary wineries trace their lineage to them. Later in the 19th century, wineries at Reuter's Hill and Helvetia made a name for the region, but neither they nor most other Oregon wineries survived Prohibition. Still, it was at Reuter's Hill that Charles Coury, one of the pioneers of the modern American wine revolution, established the first of the new Oregon wineries, in 1966. The Charles Coury Winery stayed in business for only a dozen years, but other pioneers, most notably Dick and Nancy Ponzi, persisted and their wines flourished.

■ BEAVERTON

The Beaverton woods and meadows were inhabited long before the first American settlers arrived, in 1847. The settlers planted wheat and built a gristmill, followed by a sawmill. After the railroad arrived, in 1868, the town experienced moderate growth, but it didn't really boom until the 1990s, when Hillsboro's high-tech industry expanded south, into the region now known as the Silicon Forest. Despite all this development and growth, Beaverton still has ponds inhabited by its eponymous beavers, some in waters abutting a busy freeway.

Ponzi Vineyards, the winery closest to Portland, is the first stop on our route. To get there, take U.S. 26 heading west from the city and turn south onto Route 217. Take the Route 210/Scholls Ferry Road exit and drive west, toward Scholls, about 5 miles. Shortly after the stoplight at Roy Rogers Road, you will come upon a blue highway sign indicating that you should make a left, on Vandermost Road, to reach the Ponzi winery. (If you pass an apple orchard and arrive at a flashing yellow light, turn around to find Vandermost.)

Ponzi Vineyards *map page 95, B-3*
Dick and Nancy Ponzi planted their first vineyard in 1970. By 1974 they were turning out first-rate pinot gris and pinot noir—wines they helped pioneer, and for which, along with their delightfully crisp yet full-bodied chardonnay, they've become famous.

Even though suburbia has crept to within a couple of miles, Ponzi Vineyards has one of the most beautiful settings of any Oregon winery. Shielded by a forest of

Douglas firs from winter's chilly east and north winds, the winery borders a vineyard laid out to capture the maximum warmth of the sun. Serenity reigns, and a tree-shaded patio with bistro-style chairs and tables is a fine place to linger over a glass of wine.

For the past three decades, the Ponzis have been instrumental in partnering Oregon wines and foods, working with chefs to find harmonious matches. In 1998 they opened a culinary center in Yamhill County, on Route 99W in downtown Dundee, a 30-minute drive from the vineyard. (For reservations call the Ponzi Wine Bar at 503-554-1500 or the adjacent Dundee Bistro at 503-554-1650.) *14665 SW Winery Lane; 503-628-1227. Closed Jan. and some holidays.*

After leaving Ponzi, turn left on Scholls Ferry Road. After about a quarter of a mile, turn right onto Tile Flat Road, and then, after another mile, right onto Grabhorn Road. Follow the signs to Cooper Mountain Vineyards, about 2.25 miles farther along.

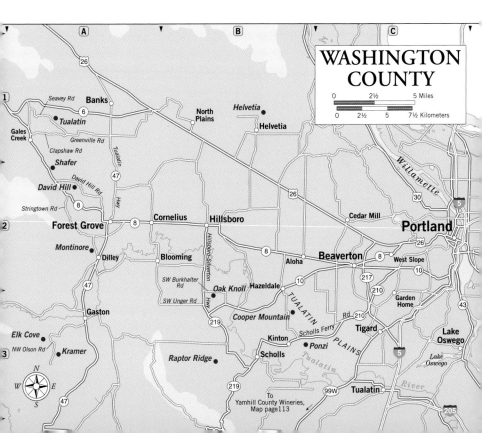

Picking berries in Hillsboro on a late summer afternoon.

Cooper Mountain Vineyards   *map page 95, B-3*

Bob Gross planted his first vines in 1978, on a south-facing slope of Cooper Mountain, an extinct volcano overlooking the Tualatin Valley. The land is notable for its uniquely shallow soils. Today, on 110 acres of certified organic vineyards—the largest organic vineyard tract in the state—Gross grows pinot gris, pinot noir, and chardonnay grapes. All the wines made here are estate-grown and produced—that is, made right here from grapes grown on the site. Over the years, Gross and his staff have developed an intimacy with every section of their vineyard, along with an understanding of how wines develop in the cellar and the bottle that has helped them capture the essence of their very special *terroir.*

Cooper Mountain Vineyards lies on a low, rolling plain framed by trees. The tasting and the picnic area have sweeping views across the vineyards and the Tualatin Valley. *9480 SW Grabhorn Road; 503-649-0027. Closed Jan. and some holidays.*

■ SCHOLLS, HILLSBORO, AND HELVETIA

Hillsboro, the Washington County seat, is a suburb of Portland best known for the Silicon Forest, the center of Oregon's computer industry. Back in the 1840s, the town's reputation was based on agricultural products. Portlanders, who have always been able to recognize good food, so appreciated Hillsboro's grain and produce that they built a plank road—a road paved with wooden planks, common in the pioneer Pacific Northwest—to Hillsboro from the Willamette, to help transport these goods to market. During World War II, Hillsboro became a bedroom community for workers flocking to Portland to aid the war effort. Intel arrived in 1970, followed by Tektronix and, throughout the 1980s, more and more high-tech companies. The suburb now sprawls over some 24 square miles in the Tualatin Valley and the Tualatin Hills. Hillsboro takes its name, incidentally, not from the hills but from the Oregon pioneer David Hill, who also gave his name to David Hill Vineyards & Winery.

From Cooper Mountain Vineyards, return to Route 210 and turn west (right); a short detour south on Route 210 will take you to Raptor Ridge Winery. After passing through the town of Scholls, turn right on Vanderschuere Road, left on Neugerbauer Road, and right on Wildhaven Lane, a gravel road.

Raptor Ridge Winery *map page 95, B-3*

The raptors—redtail hawks, sharp-shinned hawks, and kestrels—who glide above the vineyards here gave this small winery its name. Because the ridge intercepts the sea breeze, it's often foggy at Raptor Ridge. The fog cools the vineyards and imparts elusive—and highly desirable—flavor elements to the grapes, helping to produce first-rate pinot noir, pinot gris, and chardonnay. Using local grapes, the winery makes small lots of handcrafted wines with traditional Burgundian techniques, and ages the wines in French oak barrels. An unusual touch is the synchronizing of racking with the new moon, to "help bring out natural flavors and delicate aromas of Willamette Valley grapes"—though whether this timing accomplishes that end is dubious. Raptor Ridge does not use its own grapes; it buys high-quality grapes from five northern Willamette Valley vineyards. *29090 Wildhaven Lane, Scholls; 503-887-5595. Tours by appointment only, so phone ahead.*

If you don't have an appointment to visit Raptor Ridge, turn right onto Tile Flat Road after leaving Cooper Mountain, and then left onto Route 10, following it west to Burkhalter Road and Oak Knoll Winery.

Oak Knoll Winery *map page 95, B-3*

Oak Knoll was founded as a fruit-wine producer by Ron Vuylsteke, a wine-maker of Belgian ancestry, in 1970, making it one of Oregon's oldest operating wineries. Vuylsteke switched to grapes as they became more widely available, and soon Oak Knoll occupied a prime spot in the pantheon of Oregon wineries. His son, Steve Vuylsteke, now runs the operation. It's housed in an old dairy whose hollow-tile construction provides natural temperature control, but no one is taking any chances, and Oak Knoll is stocked with the latest equipment. The winery has no vineyards of its own; it purchases its grapes from reliable growers on long-term contracts. Its wines have a reputation for being food-friendly. A silky pinot noir is Oak Knoll's signature wine, but its chardonnay, pinot gris, Riesling, and gewürz-traminer are all noteworthy. Like several other Oregon wineries, Oak Knoll also makes wine from native American grapes—in this instance, niagara. *29700 SW Burkhalter Road, Hillsboro; 503-648-8198. Open daily.*

From Oak Knoll, we'll head back north to reach the next stop, Helvetia Winery. Drive west on Burkhalter Road to Route 219, turn right, and continue north into Hillsboro, turning right onto SE Oak Street/Route 8 and left onto SE 10th Street. After about 2 miles, you'll veer right (it's not a sharp turn) onto NE Cornell Road. Just after passing the Portland-Hillsboro Airport, turn left onto Brookwood Parkway, and continue straight to get onto Shute Road. After you cross U.S. 26, Shute Road becomes NW Helvetia Road. Once you've passed the Helvetia Tavern—a local landmark—turn right into Bishop Road, and then, after about a quarter of a mile, right again onto Yungen Road.

Helvetia Winery & Vineyards *map page 95, B-1*

Helvetia occupies the site of a pre-Prohibition winery founded by Jacob Yungen, a Swiss immigrant whose 100-year-old house still survives as a home. The small winery is built into a hillside, with only its front exposed—a layout that allows it to maintain a constant temperature for fermenting and aging wines. Helvetia's pinot noir, pinot gris, and chardonnay are all designed with food in mind; they go splendidly with barbecued or smoked Columbia River salmon. There's an inviting picnic area, and be sure to slip around to the cottage garden. *22485 NW Yungen Road, Helvetia; 503-647-5169. Open weekends and by appointment.*

Fresh berries for sale at Smith Berry Barn, south of Hillsboro on Scholls Ferry Road.

*(above) Montinore Vineyards' founding family, posed before the mansion they built, ca. 1904,
and the structure as it looks today (below).*
(following spread) Autumn comes to the David Hill Winery in Forest Grove.

■ FOREST GROVE

A small town spread over forested hills, Forest Grove was settled in 1840 by members of a teetotaling Christian sect who had traveled to Oregon by wagon train—which makes it something of an anomaly as a home for wineries. The young town occupied a special place among pioneer settlements because of the academy founded here in 1849, which has since grown into Pacific University. Old College Hall, built in 1850, is Oregon's oldest college building still in use. Well-maintained old homes, shady streets, and a notable lack of strip malls and other signs of urban sprawl make Forest Grove one of Oregon's prettiest towns. It took its name from a grove of Oregon white oaks that covered a prominent knoll rising above the Tualatin Valley. The name is still appropriate, and not only because the town is surrounded by forests (as well as meadows, vineyards, and wholesale plant nurseries): it now has Oregon's biggest giant sequoias—the tallest towers at more than 150 feet—in a grove planted from seeds in the 19th century.

Backtrack from the Helvetia Winery, taking Yungen Road, turning left onto Bishop Road, and taking it to Helvetia Road. Turn left, then right as Helvetia Road turns south toward U.S. 26. Cross under U.S. 26—Helvetia Road now becomes Shute Road—and follow Shute Road, continuing straight as it becomes the Brookwood Parkway. Turn right onto NE Cornell Road, then slightly left onto 10th Avenue. Turn right onto Baseline Street/Route 8 and follow Route 8 west to Forest Grove. Just before Forest Grove, look for bypass signs directing you to Route 47. Drive south on Route 47, looking for the sign directing you to Dudney Road and Montinore Estate. The winery's sign on Route 47 is hard to see, so drive slowly; it's a sharp right turn onto Dudney, and traffic on Route 47 can be heavy and fast. Make another right onto Dilley Road to reach the winery.

Montinore Estate *map page 95, A-2*

Locals chuckle at visitors who try to show off their French savvy when they pronounce "Montinore." The estate, originally a ranch, was established by a tycoon who'd made his money in the Montana mines before he retired to Oregon; he decided to call his estate *Mont*ana *in Ore*gon. The name stuck, and the winery established here three-quarters of a century later adopted it.

Montinore has 232 acres of vineyards, and its wines reflect their high quality. Highlights include a crisp gewürztraminer, a light Müller-Thurgau, an off-dry Riesling, a lush pinot noir, and a refreshing pinot gris that's a perfect partner for Northwest seafood. The tasting-room staff is among the friendliest and most

knowledgeable in Oregon Wine Country. The tasting room itself occupies the main floor of a beautiful early-20th-century mansion, set among equally beautiful gardens with picnic seating. *3663 SW Dilley Road; 503-359-5012. Open daily. Closed on some holidays.*

From Montinore, you can continue south on Route 47 to visit Elk Cove and Kramer Vineyards, the two northernmost Yamhill County wineries (see the next chapter), and then double back to continue your Washington County wine tour. Or you can reverse the trip and drop by Montinore while you're visiting Yamhill County.

To continue your tour of Washington County wineries from Montinore, turn left (north) on Dilley Road; turn left onto Springtown Road; turn right on Route 8 for the short dogleg to David Hill Road; then turn left, following the signs to the David Hill Winery. Look closely—the sign is easy to miss in rainy weather.

David Hill Vineyards & Winery *map page 95, A-2*

The David Hill Winery has splendid views of the Tualatin Valley from one of Oregon's oldest winery sites—and one with a busy past. No one has remained here for very long. It was here that, in the 19th century, the Reuter family (whose farmhouse survives as a tasting room) grew grapes and made wine, and here that Charles Coury did so much in the mid-1960s to reestablish the Oregon wine industry with his own namesake winery. After Coury left, the short-lived Reuter's Hill made light, drinkable wines, including a Riesling and a sylvaner, for a few years, until it went under. Success came with Laurel Ridge, but in 2000 that operation moved south to Yamhill County. The current enterprise produces pinot noir, chardonnay, gewürztraminer, pinot gris, Riesling, sauvignon blanc, and several Rhône blends. They're well made and pleasant, especially the eclectic blends called Farmhouse Red and Farmhouse White and the estate pinot gris; but this winery would be worth a visit for history's sake alone. *46350 NW David Hill Road; 503-992-8545. Open daily except Mon.*

From David Hill, return to Route 8 and turn right on Gales Creek Road to reach Shafer Vineyard Cellars.

Shafer Vineyard Cellars *map page 95, A-2*

This remote winery sometimes closes early, so be sure to call ahead before braving the gravel driveway, which can be hard for low-slung cars to negotiate. The rewards for making it to the top of the road are splendid views of vineyards, forests, and hills, and the chance to sip delightful chardonnay, gewürztraminer,

Photographing the vines at David Hill.

Müller-Thurgau, Riesling, pinot gris, and pinot noir. Harvey Shafer, a local builder and gentleman farmer, got into the grape business back in the early 1970s, and like others before and since, he didn't remain content with merely growing; in 1981 he started his winery. He makes wines by traditional Burgundian (i.e., slow, hands-on) methods, and the results have been consistently good. His wife, Miki, runs a year-round Christmas shop next to the tasting room. The oak-shaded picnic area has a gazebo—as welcome on a hot summer day as it is during the rainy season—that overlooks the Gales Creek Valley. *6200 NW Gales Creek Road; 503-357-6604. Open weekends Jan., daily Feb.–Dec.*

From Shafer, head west on Route 8 to Route 6. Here you can turn left and take the short drive to Tillamook and the coast. Or you can turn right and take Route 8 to U.S. 26, where a right turn—or, more precisely, a smooth merge—lands you eastbound on U.S. 26, for the return trip to Portland.

Another option would be to visit one final winery. As you leave Shafer, turn right (northwest) onto Gales Creek Road (Route 8). After not quite 6 miles, turn right onto NW Clapshaw Hill Road. Then, after about a mile and a half, turn left onto Old Clapshaw Road, which turns into Seavey Road (keep right at the T junction). Tualatin Estate will be on your left after less than a mile.

Tualatin Estate *map page 95, A-1*
This operation debuted in 1974, making it one of Oregon's pioneer wineries. But its wines have been unexciting—even a bit odd—and in 1998 the winery was acquired by Willamette Valley Vineyards, a major (for Oregon) winery corporation. Whatever you think of its wines now, Tualatin Estate is worth the short detour, because it occupies a great location, with splendid views from an umbrella-shaded picnic area. The 145-acre vineyard is planted to chardonnay, muscat, pinot blanc, and pinot noir. *10850 NW Seavey Road; 503-357-5005. Open weekends Mar.–Dec.; closed Jan.–Feb.*

Everything has its use. Grape skins and seeds left over from the crush make excellent mulch.

YAMHILL COUNTY

White Riesling grapes, ready for harvest.

IF YOU HAVE TIME TO VISIT ONLY ONE of Oregon's wine counties, it should be Yamhill County, where a happy confluence of perfect soils, a benign climate, and talented winemakers have combined to foster some superlative wines. It's about as ideal a winemaking region as you'll find anywhere in the world: warm to hot summers nourish sugars (for alcohol) and fruit (for flavor) in the grapes, and cool autumns preserve the grapes' precious acids and bring fermentation under control, maintaining the flavors and drawing out complexities. Much of the county is hilly, with north-south and east-west corridors of relatively flat land where the towns and highways are. As in California's Napa and Sonoma Counties, the vineyards are generally in the hills, the wineries on the flats.

Although vineyards flourished in the northern Willamette Valley in the 19th century, viticulture didn't arrive in Yamhill County until the 1960s and 1970s, with such pioneers as Dick Erath (Erath Vineyards Winery), David and Ginny Adelsheim (Adelsheim Vineyard), and David and Diana Lett (The Eyrie

Vineyards). The oldest and thus best-known of the county's viticultural areas is the Red Hills of Dundee, a region first planted to grapes in the 1960s. The hills' iron-rich Jory soils, derived from weathered and decomposed Columbia River basalt, are about 6 to 8 feet deep on the hillsides, making for perfect drainage, although their clays hold water late into the dry summer season.

In the 1970s, growers began planting vines in the Amity Hills, to the south. These too have volcanic soils, but generally only from 1 to 3 feet deep and containing less clay. These soils dry sooner, encouraging the fruit to ripen earlier. Some, however, have a significant clay component as well, which tends to hold moisture late into the growing season. Starting in the late 1980s, the Chehalem Mountains, to the north, and the foothills of the Coast Range, to the west, both covered with mainly Willakenzie soils, were planted to grapes. The vineyards of the Yamhill Foothills to the southwest came late to the game; their Willakenzie soils weren't planted with vines until the late 1980s.

All that stated, matters are not as clear-cut as the promotional literature sometimes suggests. A single vineyard may have several different soils. Generally speaking, the Yamhill soils are a rather confusing jumble of sedimentary and clastic debris, volcanic ash, and whatever other fragments stuck around from different geological periods.

There's more here than wine, of course. Like California's Sonoma County, Yamhill County produces a wide variety of excellent foods. The gentle slopes now planted to grapes were first cleared for fruit and nut trees, many of which are still around. The bottom lands grow magnificent vegetables. And land not suited to planting supports cattle and sheep. The few foods that aren't raised, caught, or made in the county—mostly seafood and cheese—you can get from Tillamook, on the western side of the Coast Range.

The Yamhill County wineries are only a short drive from Portland, and the roads, especially Route 99W and Route 18, can become very crowded on sunny summer weekends. (It doesn't help that these two connected roadways form one of the major highways linking Portland with the coast.) Because there are so many wineries in Yamhill County, and because their placement follows no definite pattern, this chapter has been divided into three tours.

(following pages) The magnificent soils of the Red Hills of Dundee: pinot noir vineyards at Sokol Blosser, with Domaine Drouhin in the background.

■ TOUR 1: NEWBERG TO MCMINNVILLE

This tour begins in Washington County and heads south on Route 99W to McMinnville, the Yamhill County seat and the heart of its wine country.

■ NEWBERG

After struggling through the suburban strip-mall jungle of eastern Washington County, Route 99W crosses a spur of Parrett Mountain, a 1,243-foot-high southerly extension of the Chehalem Mountains, and the landscape is magically transformed—trees, meadows, and vineyards as far as the eye can see. Look for a sign directing you to Rex Hill Winery on the right (north) side of the road.

Rex Hill Vineyards *map page 113, C-2*
A few hundred feet off the busy highway, surrounded by conifers and overlooked by vineyards, Rex Hill seems to exist in a world of its own. The winery opened in 1982, after owners Paul Hart and Jan Jacobsen converted a former nut-drying facility. It produces first-class pinot noir, pinot gris, chardonnay, sauvignon blanc, and Riesling from both estate-grown and purchased grapes. (Rex Hill owns or manages more than 225 acres of prime Willamette Valley vineyards, including holdings in the premier growing region of the Dundee Hills.) The tasting room has a massive fireplace, elegant antiques, and an absorbing collection of modern art. The landscaped, terraced gardens provide a secluded picnic spot where you can sip your wine under roses. *30835 North Highway 99W; 503-538-0666 or 800-739-4455. Open daily.*

Chehalem Winery lies across the highway from Rex Hill. Be careful when you turn onto Veritas Lane from Route 99W: cross traffic does not slow down, and there have been serious accidents here.

Chehalem Winery *map page 113, C-2*
Chehalem is a small premium winery—one of Oregon's best—with 127 acres of estate vineyards. The grapes are vinified with minimal handling, to make wines that are bold and intense, well-balanced, and full of depth—and that develop beautifully as they age. The consistently outstanding wines include pinot noir, pinot gris, chardonnay, dry Riesling and Cerise (a gamay noir–pinot noir blend). *31190 NE Veritas Lane; 503-538-4700. Open Memorial Day and Thanksgiving weekends and for special events; private tastings by appointment.*

A short distance west of Rex Hill and Chehalem, Route 99W enters Newberg proper. Yamhill County's second-largest city (after McMinnville), Newberg is surrounded by vineyards and wineries, but it's not a wine town—in fact, it was dry until after Prohibition. It was founded in the 19th century by Quakers, with the Friends Pacific Academy, now George Fox University, as a focal point, and it served as an important port on the Willamette River, from whose west bank it rises. But the railroad replaced riverboats, and the highway replaced the railroad; today Route 99W is the town's lifeline. Chehalem Creek runs through the valley north of the Red Hills of Dundee east to Newberg, where it enters the Willamette.

The surrounding area produces not only some of the United States' best wines but also 90 percent of the nation's hazelnuts. The northern Willamette Valley was also once an important center for the production of walnuts, but the local industry was already in decline by the time the Columbus Day storm of 1962 destroyed enough orchards to finish it off; it simply wasn't economically feasible to replant the trees.

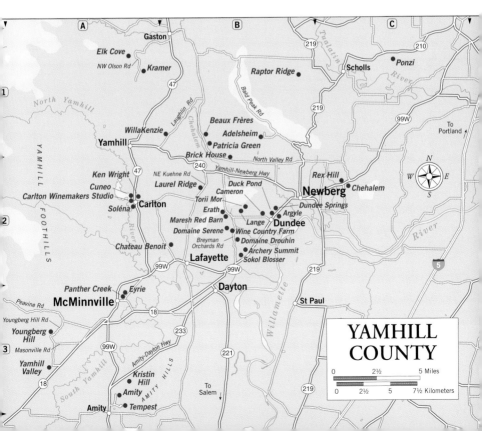

The **Ewing Young Historical Park** (Blaine Street, south end, south of East 9th Street; 503-538-7454), commemorates Ewing Young, a trapper who settled in the Chehalem Valley in 1834, near the site of modern-day Newberg. There, on Chehalem Creek, Young built the first sawmill west of the Rocky Mountains. Four buildings in the park replicate homes and cabins of Young's day. But the big draw here is decidedly in the present tense: Chehalem Skate Park. Whether Ewing Young would have appreciated this skateboarder's paradise is a matter for conjecture. But he wouldn't have minded seeing vineyards: when he set up his moonshine still, he became the first Oregonian to enter the liquor business.

Newberg's other famous citizen, Herbert Hoover, was a man of more moderate habits. Hoover came to live here with relatives from 1884 until 1889, when the family moved to Salem. The house in which he lived is now the **Hoover-Minthorne House Museum** (115 South River Street; 503-538-6629).

In a sawmill typical of those of the Yamhill County area from the 1860s through the 1880s, workers pause to pose.

■ **DUNDEE**

South of Newberg, before you reach Dundee (though technically it's just inside the Dundee town line), look for Duck Pond Cellars, on the right side of Route 99W.

Duck Pond Cellars *map page 113, B-2*

Fronted by gardens north of Route 99W, Duck Pond is one of the region's jewels. Doug and Jo Ann Fries planted the vineyards in 1986 and opened the winery in 1993. They concentrate on estate-grown Willamette Valley pinot noir and chardonnay, but also make chardonnay and merlot from grapes grown in Washington's Columbia Valley, where they have pioneered vineyard plantings on the Wahluke Slope above the Columbia River. The Duck Pond tasting room has a market that sells food and gifts, and the picnic area is a floral delight. Don't look for the duck pond, though—it's on the family ranch in eastern Oregon. *23145 Route 99W; 503-538-3199. Open daily.*

After your visit, turn right onto Route 99W. The first winery you'll see as you near town is on the right-hand side of the road. Turn right onto Fox Farm Road at the white picket fence, where the highway narrows from four lanes to two.

Dundee Springs Winery/Perry Bower Vineyard *map page 113, B-2*

This winery is sometimes called the House of Three Pinots, for its pinot noir, pinot gris, and pinot blanc, which are grown in the nearby Perry Bower estate vineyard. A demonstration vineyard familiarizes visitors with the three pinot grapes—which differ not only in color (pinot blanc and pinot gris are white, pinot noir red) but also in flavor and body, though they're actually just genetic variations of the same grape. The tasting room occupies a 1934 cottage. There are special events on Memorial Day and Thanksgiving weekends. *Route 99W and Fox Farm Road; 503-554-8000. Open Thurs.–Mon.*

The next winery, Argyle, will be on the left side of the Route 99W just as you enter Dundee proper. Look carefully for the signs to the winery, and be careful crossing the highway, especially on weekends, when traffic is heavy. The parking area is east of the winery.

Argyle Winery *map page 113, B-2*
Another beautiful establishment, Argyle has its tasting room in a Victorian farmhouse set amid gorgeous gardens. The winery is tucked into a former hazelnut processing plant—which explains the Nuthouse label on its reserve wines. Since Argyle opened in 1987, it has consistently produced sparkling wines that are crisp on the palate, with an aromatic, lingering finish and bubbles that seem to last forever. And these sparklers cost about a third of their counterparts from California. The winery also produces chardonnay, dry Riesling, pinot gris, and pinot noir. *691 North Route 99W; 503-538-8520. Open daily.*

Dundee is the last Yamhill County town on the Willamette River; a few miles below town, the Yamhill River enters from the west, and there are other towns along its banks. Dundee, you'll immediately notice, looks more like a Midwestern farm community than like its Scottish namesake. A Scotsman, William Reid, founded the town in 1874 and named it after his hometown. Early settlers planted fruit trees, and at one point Dundee was known as the Prune Capital of Oregon, but when farmers switched to hazelnuts, it became known as the Nut Town.

Today Dundee is rapidly converting itself into a wine town, and it has several first-rate restaurants. **Red Hills Provincial Dining** (276 Highway 99W; 503-538-8224) is at the east end of town; the **Dundee Bistro and Ponzi Wine Bar** (100 SW Seventh Street; 503-554-1500) are in the town center, along with **Tina's** (760 Highway 99W; 503-538-8880), an old-time restaurant with a loyal following. The **Wine Country Farm** west of town serves double duty as a B&B and winery (see page 122). At the corner of Ninth Street and Route 99W, a small shop makes superb sausages and beef jerky. (This junction is also the turnoff for several wineries in Tour 2, which begins on page 128.)

■ DAYTON

The sleepy off-highway town of Dayton was once more oriented toward the water. It was the first port on the Yamhill River, which steamboats navigated as far upriver as McMinnville. The town was founded in 1850 by Andrew Smith and Joel Palmer, on Palmer's Donation land grant. (Congress passed the Donation Land Act in 1850, to encourage westward migration and settlement of the Oregon territory.)

(top) A busy day of wine tasting at Rex Hill. (bottom) A very different tasting room: the converted Victorian farmhouse at Argyle Winery, set amid landscaped gardens.

Chef-owner Jack Czarnecki, the mushroom wizard at the Joel Palmer House in Dayton.

They named it for Smith's hometown: Dayton, Ohio. Palmer built a flour mill there, and also served as superintendent of Indian affairs for Oregon until he was fired for—believe it or not—being too lenient to the Indians.

Dayton's main attraction these days is the **Joel Palmer House,** the superb restaurant that occupies the house Palmer built for himself in 1852. The chef, Jack Czarnecki, is famous for working wonders with fresh Oregon mushrooms. He also turns out delectable meat and seafood dishes—not all of them with mushrooms, but many taking advantage of two other local commodities, hazelnuts and wine. The restaurant is on Ferry Street, but you'll look in vain for a ferry. A commercial ferry began crossing the Yamhill at Dayton in 1844, but there hasn't been ferry traffic since a bridge was built across the river in the late 19th century. *600 Ferry Street; 503-864-2995.*

You can hardly miss Sokol Blosser Winery, which rises above the vineyards to the north of Route 99W.

Sokol Blosser Winery *map page 113, B-2*

Sokol Blosser is one of Yamhill County's oldest wineries (it was established in 1977), and it makes consistently excellent wines and sells them at reasonable prices. Set on a gently sloping south-facing hillside and surrounded by vineyards, lush lawns, and shade trees and, it's a splendid place to learn about wine. A demonstration vineyard with several rows of vines contains the main grape varieties and shows what happens to them as the seasons unfold. The wines produced here include pinot noir, chardonnay, Riesling, and Müller-Thurgau. The tasting room carries charming wine gifts, and a mossy, tree-shaded picnic area below the tasting room is a fine place for cooling down and relaxing. The views across the valley are magnificent; on a clear day, Mount Jefferson, far to the east in the Cascades, looms high on the horizon. In spring, the road winding through vineyards to the winery is lined with California poppies. *5000 Sokol Blosser Lane; 503-864-2282. Open daily.*

Return to Route 99W and turn right. Off to the right is another winery—a famous one too—but it has no visitor facilities and is open by appointment only.

Domaine Drouhin Oregon *map page 113, B-2*

When the French winery magnate Robert Drouhin planted a vineyard and built a winery in the Red Hills of Dundee back in 1987, he set local enophiles abuzz. But at first this small winery, halfway up a long sunny slope, almost pretended it didn't exist, actively discouraging visitors. That attitude has changed, and you can now call for an appointment to tour the winery and taste the wines. (Be forewarned, though: this is one winery where you're expected to buy some wine if you tour, and the wines are not cheap.) As of 2003, 90 acres of the 220-acre estate had been planted. The hillside setting was selected to take advantage of the natural coolness of the earth and to establish a gravity-flow winery. The operators—the winemaker is Véronique Drouhin-Boss, from the fourth wine-making generation of the Drouhin family—say that Oregon possesses the proper climate for turning out great pinot noir, but neither Domaine Drouhin's pinot noir nor its chardonnay has achieved greatness just yet. *6750 NE Breyman Orchards Road; 503-864-2700. Tours by appointment only.*

Farther along the same road is a small winery that's far more visitor-friendly.

(following pages) Pinot noir ages in the traditional way at Archery Summit, in French oak barrels lined up in cool caves.

Wine Country Farm Cellars *map page 113, B-2*

The owners of this winery and B&B rehabilitated a neglected vineyard in the early 1990s, and pinot noir, chardonnay, Riesling and Müller-Thurgau now grow on the property. The wines made here are just right for sipping on a warm summer afternoon. The tasting room and picnic area have spectacular views of the Red Hills. You can wander over the extensive grounds, getting to know the Arabian horses, and meet Vino, the Australian shepherd. *6855 NE Breyman Orchards Road; 503-864-3446. Open daily Memorial Day–Thanksgiving, weekends the rest of the year.*

You'll need appointments to visit the next two wineries, both off Route 99W. From Wine Country Farm Cellars, backtrack south on NE Breyman Orchards Road. When it runs into Archery Summit Road, follow that road north and then east to Archery Summit Winery.

Archery Summit Winery *map page 113, B-2*

Gary and Nancy Andrus, the owners of Pine Ridge winery in the Napa Valley, started Archery Summit in the early 1990s; the first crush was in 1995. Because they believed that great wines are made in the vineyard, they adopted such innovative techniques as narrow spacing and vertical trellis systems, which give the fruit a great concentration of flavors. In addition, they did extensive clone research to develop the best possible vines for their more than 100 acres of estate vineyards. Archery Summit wines are made in a gravity-flow winery for the gentlest handling, and the wine is aged in traditional *caves*—a rarity in Oregon—in French oak barrels. The wines live up to their promise and are well worth searching out. You can tour the demonstration vineyard to learn more about the clonal studies and rootstock experimentation. *18599 NE Archery Summit Road; 503-864-4300. Open by appointment only for tastings (daily) and tours (daily except Mon.).*

About 3 miles past Dundee on Route 99W, just past the weigh station on the right, turn right on McDougall Road, and then right again on Breyman Orchards Road. After 1.7 miles, turn left on Hilltop Lane and follow it to the next winery.

Domaine Serene Vineyards and Winery *map page 113, B-2*

Established in 1989 by Ken and Grace Evenstad, this winery produces excellent pinot noir from 142 acres of vineyards on the southernmost of the Red Hills of Dundee. In a good year, the pinot noir ranks with Oregon's best; Domaine Serene also produces a delightful chardonnay. The winery, a favorite of Robert M. Parker Jr. and other wine critics, opened a five-level gravity-flow facility in 2001. *6555 NE Hilltop Lane; 503-864-4600. Open by appointment only.*

■ Lafayette

The Yamhill River meanders, and in the 19th century towns grew up at the bends of the river, where high banks offered flood protection. Dayton is on the south bank of the Yamhill; Lafayette, our next stop, is on the north. The river curves north from Dayton, and then, after lightly touching Lafayette, heads south again. The highway, Route 99W, runs almost as straight as a bow string through the Yamhill Valley, ignoring the twists in the river.

South of Route 99W, between Dayton and Lafayette, are the now-abandoned **Yamhill Locks,** which made steamer traffic to McMinnville possible by raising the level of the upper river. The locks would have made a huge difference in the development of the area in the mid-1800s, but by the end of the century, when they were finally built, railroads had made them all but superfluous. Regular steamer traffic continued on the Yamhill until about 1915, and a few boats made their way up and down river until the early 1950s, but by then the dam and locks were deteriorating badly, and a few years later the dam was removed—allowing salmon to pass upstream once again—and the lock gates taken down.

The only remnants of the locks are the 175-foot concrete walls of the lock chamber, which once gave boats a 16-foot lift over the falls here. **Lafayette Locks Park,** on the north bank (follow the signs on Route 99W), has a shaded picnic area. It's a good place for dangling your feet in the water on a sweltering day.

Lafayette, founded in 1847, is Oregon's third-oldest city, though it shows little evidence of its age, or that it was once the county seat, or even that it was laid out as a river town. It takes its name from Lafayette, Indiana, the hometown

Lafayette's old schoolhouse, built in 1912, has been turned into a mall selling antiques and collectibles.

of its founder, Joel Perkins. The first court in Yamhill County was held here, under an oak known ever after as the Council Oak. Legend has it that an elderly woman, sentenced to hang from the tree, cursed the town to burn three times. So far, it's burned only twice; superstitious residents are anxiously waiting for the third inferno.

Secluded in the wooded hills north of town is a Cistercian (Trappist) monastery, **Our Lady of Guadalupe Abbey** (503-852-0107), which plays a unique role in this part of the Oregon Wine Country. The life of contemplation and prayer to which the monks are devoted includes working in the fields, forest, and vineyards; storing, labeling, and shipping the wine of small local wineries; translating and binding books; and producing a splendid, old-style fruitcake. The monks rent rooms for spiritual retreats—four for men and four for women, though women may not pass the threshold of the cloistered area.

Before proceeding to McMinnville, we'll take a short detour into the hills to visit another winery. Though Chateau Benoit's mailing address is Carlton, it's actually much closer to Lafayette. Heading west from town on Route 99W, look for the sign directing you to Mineral Springs Road and the winery.

Chateau Benoit *map page 113, B-2*
Fred and Mary Benoit established this hilltop winery in 1979, producing Müller-Thurgau, sauvignon blanc, barrel-fermented chardonnay, pinot noir, and a dry Riesling. Several other limited-production wines are available only at the winery, including a dry gewürztraminer, a sparkling brut, and Sweet Marie dessert wine. Both the winery and picnic area have views across the hills and valleys of Yamhill County. The Benoits recently sold Chateau Benoit to Columbia Empire Farms, a local hazelnut and berry grower. So far, the new regime's results have done it honor. *6580 NE Mineral Springs Road, Carlton; 503-864-2991. Open daily.*

Return to Route 99W, heading south, and continue south when you get to Route 18. Not far from the malls and strip malls at the east end of McMinnville, the North Yamhill River comes in from the north and merges here with the South Yamhill River. The South Yamhill enters on a tortuous course from the southwest, briefly touching McMinnville after flowing past Willamina, Sheridan, and Bellevue from its source in the remote wilderness of the Coast Range.

A pastoral afternoon in the Red Hills of Dundee.

■ **McMinnville**

Known to locals as Mac, McMinnville was founded by William T. Newby, a pioneer from McMinnville, Tennessee, who came west on the Oregon Trail in 1843. In 1853 he built a gristmill at the west end of Third Street, which was the primary engine for the city's early prosperity. McMinnville's steady growth is reflected in its many well-preserved old buildings; most of the historic Third Street business buildings, which have remained remarkably unchanged, went up between 1885 and 1912. The city became the county seat in 1886.

Linfield College, near the western end of town, has a tree-shaded campus. Even though it was founded as a Baptist school, it's the site of the annual **International Pinot Noir Celebration.** An even bigger and more popular festival, though, is the July **Turkey Rama,** for which much of downtown is closed off. The events include a parade and a Biggest Turkey lip-synch contest.

McMinnville has Yamhill County's best-known restaurant, **Nick's Italian Cafe** (521 NE Third Street; 503-434-4471), which serves fixed-price five-course dinners and has one of the region's finest local wine lists.

One of Oregon's best wineries, Panther Creek Cellars, hides in downtown McMinnville, near the railroad tracks. The Eyrie Vineyards is nearby.

Panther Creek Cellars *map page 113, A-3*

Occupying a century-old structure that housed McMinnville's erstwhile power plant, this unassuming winery consistently produces some of Oregon's best pinot noirs, and—considering their high quality and the high demand—sells them at reasonable prices. The philosophy at Panther Creek is to maximize the growing process and minimize intervention, without, as the winemaker puts it, "resorting to filtering, fining, or additives." Panther Creek also makes an elegant chardonnay and an exquisite mélon de bourgogne (a grape from France's Muscadet region). The winery holds special events on Memorial Day and Thanksgiving Day weekends. *455 North Irvine Street; 503-472-8080. Open by appointment.*

The Eyrie Vineyards *map page 113, A-3*

A converted turkey-processing plant contains the Eyrie Vineyards winery, established by David and Diana Lett way back in 1966. Pinot noir, pinot gris, and chardonnay grapes are organically grown at four vineyard sites in the Dundee Hills. Unfortunately, being a pioneer does not necessarily translate into wines that are consistently good. After some initial successes, Eyrie wines have had their ups

Riesling on the vine at Yamhill Valley Vineyards.

and downs; they're generally well-made but, compared with other local wines, somewhat overpriced. *935 NE 10th Avenue; 503-472-6315. Open by appointment (call for directions) and on Thanksgiving and Memorial Day weekends.*

Southwest of town, to the northwest of Route 18, a combination B&B and winery not only provides splendid lodging but also makes some excellent wine.

Youngberg Hill Vineyards *map page 113, A-3*

Nestled amid the Coast Range foothills, Youngberg Hill's vineyards, with spectacular views of the Willamette Valley, are also the setting for an elegant inn. This boutique winery, established in 1996, produces an average of 600 cases of pinot noir a year. The vineyard, at elevations ranging from 650 to 700 feet, is not irrigated, which causes the vines to struggle to produce grapes. The resulting stress helps the grapes that do grow to develop more complex flavors. The soil is mainly Willakenzie, which dries hard in the summer without any rains. The winery is open by appointment (and to anyone who stays at the inn), and there are special events on Thanksgiving Day and Memorial Day weekends. *10660 SW Youngberg Hill Road; 503-472-2727.*

■ TOUR 2: THE RED HILLS AND CHEHALEM

This long tour takes us from Dundee to wineries high in the Red Hills and on to wineries in the rustic Chehalem Valley to the north, heading to the small towns of Yamhill, Gaston, and Carlton, and finishing with an optional visit to four interesting but seldom-open wineries.

■ DUNDEE

Driving on Route 99W in downtown Dundee, turn onto Ninth Street (right if you're coming from Newberg, left if you're coming from McMinnville) and continue uphill. And stick to the speed limit, or this trip could become expensive. Ninth Street soon turns into Worden Hill Road. The Cameron Winery is marked by a large sign in a vineyard to the right.

Per Hatting, the tasting room manager at Torii Mor, pours one for himself. Torii Mor's Japanese-garden setting is spectacular.

Cameron Winery *map page 113, B-2*
It's difficult to improve on the poetic style of the blurb on this winery's brochure, so here it is unaltered:

> With irreverent newsletters, no organizational skills and outrageous prices, it's amazing that this vigneron has managed to stay in business for 15 years. Because of government cutbacks to the National Park System, Cameron found it necessary to close its doors to the public on all weekends except Thanksgiving. That weekend, however, they'll hide the free-range chickens, scrub their fingernails and offer wines from four distinctive vineyards: Abbey Ridge, Brick House and Clos Electrique, and Croft.

Winemaker Jean Paul, a veteran of many different vineyards and wine regions, knows his craft. He makes pinot noir and chardonnay in small lots and distributes them locally. *8200 Worden Hill Road; 503-538-0336. Open Thanksgiving weekend.*

If you've stopped at Cameron, return to Worden Hill Road and turn right. Look for Fairview Road and turn right on it. Torii Mor Winery is up the hill on the right.

Torii Mor Winery *map page 113, B-2*
Torii Mor, established in 1993, makes small quantities of hand-crafted pinot noir, pinot gris, and chardonnay. The tasting room, at the surrounding Olson Vineyard, one of Yamhill County's oldest vineyards, has an amazing setting amid Japanese gardens with breathtaking views of the Willamette Valley. The owners, who love things Japanese, named their winery after the distinctive Japanese gate of Shinto religious significance; they added a Scandinavian *mor,* signifying "earth," to create an east-west combo: "earth gate." Joe Dobbes has replaced Patricia Green (who left to open her own winery nearby—see page 136) as winemaker. *18325 NE Fairview Drive; 503-538-2279. Open Fri.–Sun.*

After leaving Torii Mor, continue uphill on Fairview Drive to Buena Vista. Turn right to reach Lange Winery, tucked into trees atop a knoll.

Lange Winery *map page 113, B-2*
Don and Wendy Lange moved north from Santa Barbara, California, in 1987, and planted their first vineyard in 1988, in pursuit of first-rate pinot noir. They now produce it: their wines (which also include pinot gris and chardonnay) are consistently complex and well balanced, and they have depth. Some of Lange's

pinot noir comes from a 15-acre estate vineyard; other grapes come from local growers. Lange makes two styles of pinot noir: a traditional vat-fermented wine and a more complex barrel-fermented wine. The winery has astounding views of the Willamette and Chehalem Valleys. *18380 NE Buena Vista; 503-538-6476. Open daily except Tues.*

Return to Worden Hill Road and turn right. Keep an eye out for a red barn in a grove of trees atop a knoll to the left. This marks Maresh Red Barn, a winemaking landmark.

Maresh Red Barn *map page 113, B-2*

When Jim and Loie Maresh planted two acres of vines in 1970, theirs became the fifth vineyard in Oregon and the first on Worden Hill Road. The quality of their grapes was so high that some of the region's best and most famous wineries were soon searching them out. When the wine industry boomed in the 1980s, the Mareshes decided they might as well make some wine from their renowned grapes. They transformed their old barn into a tasting room—which is the only place you can purchase Red Barn's exceptional chardonnay, pinot noir, and white Riesling. *9325 NW Worden Hill Road; 503-537-1098. Open Thurs.–Sun. Closed Jan.*

Turn left (west) onto Worden Hill Road as you leave Maresh. After passing hillside vineyards with some splendid views, the road dips into a draw and turns northwest. At the bottom of the draw, a sign directs you to both Crabtree Park and Erath Vineyards Winery. Turn left. Erath is on the more westerly road; the entrance to the park is more southerly—but they're basically at the same intersection. There are excellent, highly visible signs to direct you.

Erath Vineyards Winery *map page 113, B-2*

One of Oregon's pioneer wineries, Erath Vineyards opened more than a quarter of a century ago. Its owner and winemaker, Dick Erath, has focused on producing distinctive pinot noir from grapes he's been growing in the Red Hills since 1972—as well as full-flavored pinot gris, pinot blanc, chardonnay, cabernet sauvignon, Riesling, and late-harvest gewürztraminer. The wines are not only excellent but reasonably priced too. The tasting room is in the middle of the vineyards, high in the hills, with views in nearly every direction: the hazelnut trees that covered the slopes not so long ago have been replaced with vines. The tasting-room terrace, which overlooks the winery and the hills, is a choice spot for picnicking. *9409 NE Worden Hill Road; 503-538-3318. Open daily.*

Crabtree Park, next to the winery, is a good place to stretch your legs after a tasting. To get to the next winery, turn left (north) onto Worden Hill Road. After a short distance, gravel replaces the pavement; it's still easy to navigate, but watch out for flying rocks and, on busy summer days, dust. Follow Worden Hill Road for about 2.75 miles to Route 240. Turn left and follow the highway 7-plus miles to Laughlin Road. Turn right; you'll reach WillaKenzie Estate in a little less than a mile and a half.

■ CHEHALEM VALLEY

WillaKenzie Estate *map page 113, A-1*
The vineyards on this 400-acre estate are set amid the Chehalem Valley's rolling hills and surrounded by Douglas firs. The winery's dramatic gravity-feed facility, completed in 1995, has three levels, including a large underground barrel room. WillaKenzie combines modern technology with traditional wine-making methods to produce excellent pinot noir, pinot gris, and pinot blanc. Visitor amenities include a bistro-style tasting room, a self-guided tour of the winery, and a scenic picnic area looking out to the vineyards and the mountains. *19143 NE Laughlin Road, Yamhill; 503-662-3280. Open Memorial Day–Labor Day; Fri.–Sun. the rest of the year.*

After leaving WillaKenzie Estate, turn right onto Laughlin Road, left onto Route 240, then right into NE Kuehne Road and follow the signs to Laurel Ridge Winery.

Laurel Ridge Winery *map page 113, B-2*
This establishment moved south from Washington County a few years back but quickly hit its stride in Yamhill County, producing top-notch pinot noir and port from its Finn Hill Vineyard. Laurel Ridge also makes sauvignon blanc, chardonnay, Riesling, sparkling wines, and pinot gris. The state-of-the-art winery is housed in a late-19th-century barn building, and the well-designed tasting room overlooks a traditional country setting. *13301 NE Kuehne Road, Carlton; 503-852-7050. Open daily.*

From Laurel Ridge, return to Route 240, turn left onto it, and drive into Yamhill, a small city that has so far escaped wine-boom gentrification. A handful of old business buildings line the main drag, Route 47; a few 19th-century mansions rise over quiet gardens on the side streets; and that's about it. The **Yamhill Cafe**

(240 South Maple Street; 503-662-3504) specializes in comfort food. From Yamhill, turn north onto Route 47 and follow it almost all the way to Gaston, a small town across the county line in Washington County. Turn left on NW Olson Road, which winds along a ridge and takes you to the Elk Cove Vineyards.

Elk Cove Vineyards   *map page 113, A-1*

If you look out across the vineyards from Elk Cove's tasting room, you can make out the small, weathered barn where Pat and Joe Campbell started making wine back in 1978. (They had planted their first vineyard in 1973, in a sunny, secluded corner of the North Willamette Valley.) Their excellent wines include pinot noir, pinot gris, chardonnay, Riesling (dry and late-harvest), cabernet sauvignon, and Ultima dessert wines. They got the name Elk Cove from the Roosevelt elk that once migrated into the valley each spring. *27751 NW Olson Road, Gaston; 503-985-7760. Open daily.*

From Elk Cove, turn right into Olson Road. Kramer Vineyards is a bit farther along on the left-hand side.

Kramer Vineyards   *map page 113, A-1*

Keith and Trudy Kramer got the idea of opening a winery when Trudy's homemade raspberry wine won a gold medal two decades ago at the Oregon State Fair. They planted a vineyard in 1984, taking a further plunge with a winery in 1990, and they've succeeded spectacularly. Trudy's vinifera wines rank with the best produced in Oregon. Kramer Vineyards produces pinot noir, merlot, syrah, chardonnay, pinot gris, Riesling, and Müller-Thurgau. The picnic deck is framed by native shrubs and trees and has views over the valley below. *26830 NW Olson Road, Gaston; 503-662-4545. Open Fri.–Sun. Mar.–Dec., daily June–Sept.; closed Jan.–Feb.*

Return to Route 47, turn right, and head south. In countryside dotted with plant nurseries you'll come into downtown Carlton. Several old brick buildings line Main Street, and along the side streets are a few 19th-century gingerbread mansions. The popular **Caffe Bisbo** (214 West Main Street; 503-852-7248) serves northern Italian dishes.

Go west on Main Street, crossing South Yamhill Street/Route 47, to Scott Street, and turn right. Carlton Winemakers Studio is in the next block.

A polite but firm warning to visitors at Kramer Vineyards in Gaston.

Carlton Winemakers Studio *map page 113, A-2*
Oregon's first cooperative winery was specifically designed to house multiple small, premium wine producers. This gravity-flow winery has up-to-date wine-making equipment as well as multiple cellars for storing the different makers' wines. Visitors can taste and purchase bottles from Andrew Rich Vintner (cabernet franc, cabernet sauvignon, grenache, malbec, pinot noir, syrah, chenin blanc, gewürztraminer, sauvignon blanc, and Rhône blends); Domain Meriwether (pinot noir); Hamacher Wines (pinot noir, chardonnay, and a dry pinot noir rosé); Penner-Ash Wine Cellars (pinot noir, syrah, viognier); Bryce Vineyards (pinot noir and viognier); and other wineries. *801 North Scott Street, Carlton; 503-852-6100. Open Wed.–Sun. in late spring, summer, and early fall, with scaled back hours at other times. Closed Jan.*

Return to Route 47 and follow it south to the next winery. (After turning south from Main Street at a four-way stop, Route 47 follows Pine Street.)

Kramer Vineyards' vinifera wines rank among Oregon's best.

Soléna *map page 113, A-2*

This small winery originated in the passion of two seasoned Yamhill County enologists. Laurent Montalieu was the winemaker at WillaKenzie Estate; Danielle Andrus Montalieu ran her family's Archery Summit winery. The two got married in 2002, opened a winery of their own the same year, and had a daughter in 2003; they named both the winery and the daughter Soléna. Visit the tasting room and the cellar to sample cabernet sauvignon, merlot, pinot noir, syrah, and zinfandel from the bottle and the barrel. *213 South Pine Street, Carlton; 503-662-3149. Open Thurs.–Sun., Sat. only in winter.*

Cuneo Cellars *map page 113, A-2*

This outfit got its start in 1993 when Gino and Pam Cuneo bought a winery in the Eola Hills. In 2001 they moved Cuneo Cellars into a new winery, a Tuscan-inspired building north of Carlton on Route 47. That was phase one of an ambitious building project. Phase two, which should be completed by 2006, involves landscaping the grounds according to a similar Italian theme; they've already planted olive trees. Though the old winery occupied a lovely site in the Eola Hills,

they needed the new building to make room for barrel storage of their Bordeaux and Italian varietals. Cuneo currently produces pinot noir, syrah, sangiovese, and nebbiolo. A bocce ball court (naturally) and a picnic area invite visitors to linger. *750 Lincoln Street, Carlton; 503-852-0002. Open daily.*

Ken Wright Cellars *map page 113, A-2*
The operators of this small winery, tucked into a Carlton backstreet, go to great pains to protect the inherent qualities of the grapes they have gathered from the vineyards under contract to them. Carefully selected sites, severe limitations on crop level, and thorough hand-sorting all play a part in the process. Besides pinot noir from grapes grown in the Dundee Hills, Eola Hills, and Coast Range, Ken Wright also produces limited quantities of three white wines: chardonnay from the Celilo Vineyard in the Columbia Gorge near White Salmon, Washington; Dijon 76, a clone of chardonnay from Yamhill County; and pinot blanc from Freedom Hill Vineyard in the Coast Range south of Dallas, Oregon. *236 North Kutch Street, Carlton; 503-852-7070. Open by appointment only.*

■ **NORTHWEST OF NEWBERG**
From Carlton, you can call it a day and drive south on Route 47 to return to McMinnville. Or you can continue the tour by visiting four interesting wineries that are open only by appointment or on special occasions. To reach them, drive north from Carlton to Yamhill; then turn right onto Route 240, the Newberg-Yamhill Highway. All four wineries lie north of Route 240. (Since it's likely that you'll be visiting them at different times, we've supplied directions for continuing Tour 2 from Yamhill and alternate directions for reaching these wineries from Newberg on another day.)

To get to the first one, Patricia Green Cellars, if you're coming from Yamhill, follow Route 240 east for about 6 miles, to Ribbon Ridge Road, and turn left (north). At the junction (a little more than three quarters of a mile), make a sharp left onto NE North Valley Road. Patricia Green Cellars will appear after about 2 miles. (If you're coming from Newberg, take Route 240 west to Ribbon Ridge Road—about 5.5 miles—and turn right, or north; after less than a mile, turn left onto NE North Valley Road.)

Patricia Green Cellars *map page 113, B-1*

Patricia Green, the former winemaker for Torii Mor Winery, and her cellar master, James Anderson, bought and renamed the Autumn Wind Winery in April 2000. So far, they've made pinot noir from some of the region's best vineyards, including Shea, Balcombe, Quail Hill, and their own estate vineyard. So far they are achieving their goal of producing estate-bottled pinot noirs that are well-balanced, dense, complex, distinct, and enjoyable. The winery also makes a sauvignon blanc and has experimented with pinot noirs made from California grapes. *15225 NE North Valley Road, Newberg; 503-554-0821. Open Memorial Day and Thanksgiving weekends and by appointment.*

After leaving Patricia Green cellars, continue north on NE North Valley Road to Beaux Frères.

Beaux Frères *map page 113, B-1*

This winery is noteworthy partly because one of its owners is the internationally renowned wine critic Robert M. Parker Jr.; the co-owners are his wife, Pat, her younger brother, Michael Etzel, and Michael's wife, Jackie. They offer wine under several labels, including the flagship single-vineyard-designate Beaux Frères, made from their organically grown estate pinot noir. They produce additional wines under a sister label, Belles Soeurs, made out of grapes purchased from some of Oregon's top vineyards. *15155 NE North Valley Road, Newberg; 503-537-1137. Open Memorial Day and Thanksgiving weekends only.*

From Beaux Frères, turn south on NE North Valley Road and return to the junction with Ribbon Ridge Road. Make a sharp left (north) and follow Ribbon Ridge Road for about three quarters of a mile to Lewis Rogers Lane and Brick House Vineyards. (If you're coming from Newberg, take Route 240 west for 4 miles; turn right on Dopp Road; turn left at NE North Valley Road; turn right on Lewis Rogers Lane and drive to the last mailbox.)

Brick House Vineyards *map page 113, B-1/2*

Brick House's 30 acres of vineyards—planted to pinot noir, chardonnay, and gamay noir—surround a 1920s brick house and barn that, restored, serve as the winery. It was founded in 1990 by Doug Tunnell, a former television newsman whose vine-planting philosophy is simple and telling: "Plant them in shallow

Adventure seekers about to get a bird's-eye view of Yamhill County.

soils on a hillside and give them the morning sun. Don't plow too much. Don't hoe too much. Let them struggle. And don't ever forget: the world's finest fertilizer is the footprint of the winegrower . . . in the mud of March and the dust of September." All Brick House wines are estate grown, certified organic, and produced and bottled on the property. And they're superb. *18200 Lewis Rogers Lane, Newberg; 503-538-5136. Open Thanksgiving weekend and by appointment.*

From Brick House Vineyards, make a sharp left onto Ribbon Ridge Road. After about three quarters of a mile, turn left onto NE Calkins Lane. Drive east for almost a mile and a half to reach Adelsheim Vineyard. (If you're coming from Newberg, turn right, or north, on Main Street/Route 240. After about 2.8 miles, turn right on Stone Road, which ends 0.9 miles later, at its intersection with NE North Valley Road. Turn left and go 1.2 miles, turning right onto NE Calkins Lane. The winery's gate is 0.6 miles farther along.)

Adelsheim Vineyard *map page 113, B-1*
David Adelsheim is the knight in shining armor of the Oregon wine industry—tirelessly promoting Oregon wines abroad, and always willing to share the knowledge he has gained from his long viticultural experience. He and Ginny Adelsheim founded their pioneer winery nearby in 1971; their present winery was completed in 1997. They make most of their wines from grapes picked on their 165 acres of estate vineyards. Their pinot noir, pinot gris, pinot blanc, and chardonnay all conform to the Adelsheim house style, with rich, balanced fruit and long, clean finishes. They also make a dessert wine, Deglace, from pinot noir grapes. In the spring of 2003, they released wine from a grape entirely new to Oregon: tocai friulano, a refreshing and flavorful white that's in a league with the best that the Friuli region of northern Italy has to offer. Adelsheim wines are widely available in restaurants and wine shops throughout the Northwest. *16800 NE Calkins Lane, Newberg; 503-538-3652. Open by appointment only.*

From Adelsheim, turn left (west) onto Calkins Lane. After a little more than half a mile, turn left onto Dopp Road, and follow it south to Route 240 (about 2.5 miles). Once you reach Route 240, turn right to return to Yamhill or left to reach Newberg.

Grapes aren't all that flourishes at Yamhill Valley Vineyards.

■ Tour 3: The Amity Hills and the Coast Range Foothills

This final Yamhill County tour takes you in a loop from McMinnville south to the Amity Hills, then back by way of Route 18 and the Coast Range foothills. Driving south on Route 99W, you'll come upon the first winery almost unexpectedly. The hills sneak up on you as they suddenly rise from the valley—it's a case of not being able to see the hills for the trees—at the corner of Route 99W and the Amity-Dayton Highway. Look for signs; the winery is on the left.

■ Amity

Kristin Hill Winery *map page 113, A-3*

The Aberg family planted its first vineyard in 1985, with the help of family and friends, and established this winery in 1990. It has achieved quite a bit of acclaim since then. Kristin Hill's best seller is a traditional *méthode champenoise* sparkling wine. But its Alsatian-style gewürztraminer, chardonnay, pinot noir, pinot gris, Riesling, and, in a softer vein, Müller-Thurgau are all worth sampling. The ambience is very laid back; bring a picnic lunch, sit out on the deck on a sunny afternoon, and listen to the birds as you enjoy the wines. *3330 SE Amity-Dayton Highway; 503-835-0850. Open daily Mar.–Dec. 21, weekends and by appointment Dec. 26–Feb.*

Return to Route 99W, turn left (south), and continue into Amity. The town was founded in 1849 and got its name after a fierce fight over the site for a school ended in amicable agreement. But in recent years the town hasn't lived up to the name: in 2000, the city council fired the city manager; in retaliation, voters recalled three city council members.

On the weekend prior to spring break, Amity High School students organize the annual Daffodil Festival; most of the events (flower and art shows, music, runs and walks, plant and garden-product sales, gardening-related presentations) take place at Amity Elementary School. Downtown Amity has several antiques shops, a café, and not much else. It's the nearby wineries that have put the town on the map. Well, the wines and the as-seen-on-TV Brigittine Monks Gourmet Fudge, produced by the residents of **Priory of Our Lady of Consolation** (23300 SW Walker Lane; 503-835-8080).

From Route 99W in town, head west on Rice Road, which becomes Rice Lane. Follow the signs up the hill—the gravel road is steep and curvy—to the next winery.

Amity Vineyards *map page 113, A-3*

Everyone seems like family at this small, pioneering winery—it dates back to 1976—perched on a slope overlooking the Willamette Valley and the Coast Range foothills. But its easygoing attitude doesn't get in the way of wine that's consistently among Oregon's best. Winemaker Myron Redford specializes in traditional barrel-aged pinot noir; he also turns out an "Eco" wine—a sulfite-free pinot noir made from organically grown grapes—that's utterly delicious. Other varietals include a smooth, dry pinot blanc; both dry and late-harvest gewürztraminer and Riesling; a gamay noir; and a delectable rosé he calls Oregon Blush. The barebones picnic area has, in addition to splendid views, a fig tree Redford brought down with him from Seattle—and, yes, it bears luscious fruit. *18150 Amity Vineyards Road; 503-835-2362. Open daily Feb.–Dec. 23; closed Dec. 24–Jan. 31.*

From Amity Vineyards, turn left (east) onto Rice Lane and drive to the end; then turn right onto Karla's Road and continue to Tempest Vineyards.

Tempest Vineyards *map page 113, A-3*

Tempest Vineyards, a very little, almost secretive family-owned winery, produces small quantities of notable pinot noir, chardonnay, and a few other varieties, and four aperitif wines, using traditional methods of minimal handling and long barrel aging. It's tucked into a rather steep wooded slope of the Amity Hills (east of Amity) and is open only four times a year. *6000 Karla's Road, Amity; 503-835-2600. Open four weekends—the first weekend after Apr. 15, Memorial Day, Labor Day, and Thanksgiving—and by appointment.*

Return to Route 99W and turn left (south); turn right onto SW Bellevue Road and follow this road to Bellevue; then turn right onto Route 18 and look for signs directing you to Yamhill Valley Vineyards. Finally, turn left onto SW Oldsville Road and follow it to the winery.

(following pages, counter-clockwise from bottom right) Three of the many wine-making steps at Amity Vineyards: bringing in the crush, sorting the grapes, and checking the sugar content of the must.

■ McMinnville

Yamhill Valley Vineyards *map page 113, A-3*
Yamhill Valley Vineyards released its first vintage in 1983. The estate vineyard, on a rolling 300-acre spread in the foothills of the Coast Range, produces pinot noir, pinot gris, pinot blanc, chardonnay, and Riesling grapes with a rich varietal character; the winery taps their full potential with traditional wine-making practices, but without shunning modern equipment and techniques. Part of the wines' success is based, no doubt, on the vineyards' complex array of the best Willamette Valley soils. The winery has a pleasant picnic area. *16250 SW Oldsville Road; 800-825-4845. Open weekends mid-Mar.–May, daily June–Nov. Closed Dec.–mid-Mar.*

A final note: if you drive south on SW Oldsville Road after leaving Yamhill Valley Vineyards, you'll see a sign marked **"Glacial Erratic."** You can pull over and park on the shoulder to see a huge boulder rafted here during the Ice Age Spokane Floods. It's said to be the largest boulder to have traveled this far from the Montana bedrock.

Regular rows of carefully pruned Willamette Valley vines.

SALEM AREA

IT SEEMS AT TIMES THAT THE WILLAMETTE VALLEY is more hills than valley, and nowhere is this more the case than near the state capital, Salem, with the Eola Hills to the west and northwest, the Salem Hills to the south, and the Waldo Hills to the east and northeast—not to mention the towering mountains of the Coast Range and the Cascades to either side. Many of these hills have perfect soils and perfect microclimates for nurturing grapes. So far most of the region's vineyards have been planted in the Eola Hills west of the Willamette River, perhaps as spillover from the highly successful Yamhill County wineries to the north. Eola is a corruption of Aeolus, the god of winds; the hills get their name from the winds blowing up and down the valley across the rounded slopes of the ridges.

Today's isn't the first Eola Hills alcohol boom. During Prohibition, the hills were a haven for moonshiners. Grape growing and wine-making here date back further. In the 1830s, French-Canadian trappers who had retired from the Hudson's Bay Company planted the region's first wine grapes on the slopes of La Butte, one of the many weathered volcanic plugs dotting the valley.

The iron-rich red soils of the Eola Hills consist of the same decomposed Columbia River basalts as in the Red Hills of Dundee, but they're shallower—a mere 1 to 3 feet deep as compared to the Red Hills' 6 to 8 feet. They also contain less clay, though they still have enough to hold moisture late into the season. Because the soil dries out a bit sooner, growers must encourage the fruit to ripen earlier—as the 19th-century pioneers discovered, to their dismay, when they had difficulty getting the fruit in their wind-swept orchards to ripen properly. The hot sun and warm winds of summer nurture sugars in the grapes, adding complex flavors to chardonnay; the cool, windy, sunny days of fall enhance acids, not only adding structure and stability to chardonnay but also yielding full-flavored, pleasingly tart pinot gris. But there are many different soils and microclimates here, and the Eola Hills also produce world-class pinot noir.

For convenience, this chapter has been divided into two tours. The first begins in Salem and heads west; the second travels in the opposite direction. It's possible to do both tours in a single day.

A boy atop Big Sky, one of the hand-carved ponies on the carousel in Salem's Riverfront Park. The old-fashioned ride, the result of community action and volunteer labor, opened in 2001.

■ TOUR 1: SALEM AND THE EOLA HILLS

■ SALEM

This beautiful, laid-back city on the Willamette River has deep wine-making roots. From Prohibition to the wine boom of the late 1900s, Oregon's capital was also Oregon's wine capital—all because of one winery, Honeywood. There are lots of attractions, of course: the **State Capitol** (900 Court Street NE; 503-986-1388) and its beautiful grounds; the **Bush House Museum and Conservatory** (600 Mission Street SE; 503-363-4714); **Mission Mill Museum** (1313 Mill Street SE; 503-585-7012); and many parks, including Riverfront Park, graced by the new but old-fashioned **Riverfront Carousel** (Front and State Streets; 503-540-0374).

Salem has several excellent restaurants and hotels, which make it a fine base for exploring the Eola Hills wine country and several outlying wineries—most of which are also within reach of Newberg and McMinnville (see the "Yamhill County" chapter) to the north. The state capital is a beer and cocktail town, but two good bets for wine are **Alessandro's 120** (120 Commercial Street NE; 503-391-1774), which has been around for a long time and may have the best wine list in town; and **McGrath's Fish House** (350 Chemeketa Street NE; 503-362-0736).

Honeywood Winery lies south of downtown Salem and just south of Mission Street (Route 22), on Hines Street off 13th Street. From Mission Street (Route 22), turn south into 12th Street, then left (east) onto Hines. Look for the winery on the left, just after the railroad tracks.

Honeywood Winery *map page 149, C-3*
Established in 1934, right after Prohibition ended, Honeywood is the oldest continuously producing winery in Oregon. In the early years, its wines came not from grapes but from the berries that thrive in the Willamette Valley. Honeywood still has the most extensive repertoire of premium fruit and specialty wines in Oregon, including such classics as plum, blackberry, raspberry, loganberry, and rhubarb. But the winery, recognizing changing tastes, has now branched into vinifera wines, including pinot noir, Riesling, chardonnay, muscat, and gewürztraminer—although some of these wines are blended with fruit flavors. Honeywood has a loyal following, and you'll see why after you taste the wines, which are surprisingly complex. Be sure to sample the blackberry, Honeywood's best seller, and the truly splendid red currant, which goes beautifully—if surprisingly—with grilled salmon. *1350 Hines Street SE; 503-362-4111. Open daily.*

Return to Mission Street (Route 22) from Hines Street by turning right onto 13th Street and following the signs to Route 22. Continue west on Route 22 across the Willamette River and turn right (north) onto Route 221 (Wallace Road NW). Evesham Wood lies about half a mile north of the turnoff.

Evesham Wood Winery *map page 149, B-2*

This small family winery at the southern end of the Eola Hills is one of Oregon's best, which explains why its reasonably priced wines are so hard to find: restaurants, wine shops, and aficionados on the winery's mailing list snap them up as soon as they're released. The winemaker, Russ Raney, is a kind, unassuming man whom quite a few enophiles regard as a genius. His best pinot noirs are elegant, silky, and deeply complex; happily, he has recently increased their production. He also produces deeply rich chardonnay and exquisite pinot gris. *3795 Wallace Road NW; 503-371-8478. By appointment only.*

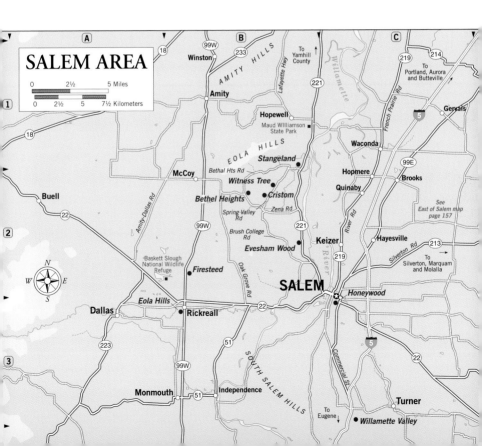

From Evesham Wood, continue north on Route 221 for about 2.5 miles, to Zena Road. Turn left (west); then, after about 2.25 miles, turn right onto Spring Valley Road NW to reach Cristom Vineyards another mile farther along.

Cristom Vineyards *map page 149, B-2*
Paul and Eileen Gerrie had a vision of making handcrafted wines, and in 1992 they planted vineyards to pinot noir, pinot gris, chardonnay, and viognier. These estate grapes are carefully crushed by winemaker Steve Doerner, fermented with native yeasts, and moved from fermenter to vat and barrels by gravity flow. The wines are aged in subterranean cellars with a naturally even temperature, then left unfiltered for extra depth and complexity; and they have gained a following. The winery and tasting room overlook the Eola Hills. *6905 Spring Valley Road NW; 503-375-3068. Open Fri.–Sun. and by appointment.*

North up Spring Valley Road NW from Cristom lies Witness Tree Vineyard.

The estate vineyards at Witness Tree, overlooking the Eola Hills.

Witness Tree Vineyard *map page 149, B-2*

Witness Tree takes its name from an ancient Oregon oak rising above the vineyard. This oak already stood tall when the first American pioneers arrived in the Willamette Valley in the 19th century; it was used as a surveyor's landmark as far back as 1854, when the first farms were laid out in the then-wild hills. The winery overlooks the southern Eola Hills from its 100-acre estate vineyard, whose first vines were planted in 1980. Pinot noir, chardonnay, pinot blanc, and viognier are all made here from estate-grown grapes. *7111 Spring Valley Road NW; 503-585-7874. Open Tues.–Sun. June–Aug., weekends Mar.–May and Sept.–Dec. Closed except on holiday weekends Jan.–Feb.*

Taking Spring Valley Road to its northern end will bring you to Hopewell Road NW and Stangeland Vineyards.

Stangeland Vineyards *map page 149, B-1*

Overlooking the Eola Hills from a sunny southern slope, Stangeland is a quintessential Oregon winery. The owners, Larry and Kinsey Miller, produce pinot noir, pinot gris, chardonnay, and gewürztraminer along with two proprietary blends, most of these wines unfined and unfiltered. The winery takes its name from the couple's Norwegian heritage; their grandparents on both sides were Norwegian immigrants. In Norwegian, *stangeland* means, roughly, "stony ground"—an apt description of the land here. *8500 Hopewell Road NW; 503-581-0355. Open weekends May–Nov., the first weekend of the month Dec.–Apr., and by appointment.*

If the day is hot and you'd like to relax in the shade of tall trees, drive east from Stangeland on Hopewell Road NW to Route 221 and turn left (north). Look for the signs directing you to **Maud Williamson State Park** (Route 221, just southwest of SE Lafayette Highway), about 3 miles north of the intersection. The basic amenities here include green lawns, picnic tables, rest rooms, and giant, shade-giving Douglas firs.

To continue touring from Stangeland, turn left onto Hopewell Road NW. After about a quarter of a mile, turn right onto Route 221, and drive south to Zena Road. Turn right (west); then, after about 3.5 miles, turn right again onto Bethel Heights Road NW. Follow the signs to Bethel Heights Vineyard, which is on the right side of the road about 500 yards from the intersection.

At Bethel Heights Vineyards, the focus is on pinot noir.

Sorting grapes at Bethel Heights.

Bethel Heights Vineyard

map page 149, B-2

When it was planted back in 1977, Bethel Heights Vineyard was a pioneer; today its 51-acre vineyard is one of many in the Eola Hills. The winery itself was finished in 1984. The focus here is on pinot noir; more than half of the estate vineyard is planted to that Burgundian red-wine grape, and Bethel Heights produces several different bottlings each year. (As is typical among Willamette Valley wineries, it also turns out some wines from purchased grapes.) These wines get their rich flavors from warm fermentation, with the help of wild yeasts and from aging in small French oak barrels for 10 to 18 months. The wines are racked as little as possible, and they're usually bottled unfiltered. Bethel Heights also produces chardonnay, pinot blanc, and pinot gris from estate-grown grapes. The tasting room and picnic area have sweeping views of Spring Valley and of Mount Jefferson, far to the east in the High Cascades. *6060 Bethel Heights Road NW; 503-581-2262. Open Tues.–Sun. June–Aug., weekends Mar.–May and Sept.–Nov.; closed Dec.–Feb. except by appointment.*

■ RICKREALL

After visiting Bethel Heights, continue south on Bethel Heights Road NW; turn right (west) onto Zena Road and follow it, as it becomes Bethel Road, to Route 99W. Turn left onto Route 99W; just beyond the junction of Route 99W and Route 22, you'll spot Eola Hills Wine Cellars on the right-hand side of the road.

Eola Hills Wine Cellars *map page 149, B-3*

The name is a bit of a misnomer, since this winery isn't actually in the Eola Hills, which lie a couple of miles to the northeast, but in the crossroads village of Rickreall. Its vineyards spread out over the hills of the northwestern Willamette Valley, and the winery, which opened in 1988, sits right in the middle. Wines to look for here include cabernet sauvignon, pinot noir, merlot, chardonnay, pinot gris, gewürztraminer, and Riesling, as well as late-harvest dessert wines. Eola Hills also produces a number of private-label wines for restaurants and other clients. It's locally famous for its Sunday brunches (reservations are essential), which have taken food-and-wine pairings to new heights. *501 South Pacific Highway (Route 99W); 503-623-2405. Open daily.*

Leaving Eola Hills Wine Cellars, turn left (north) onto Route 99W. Just beyond the Route 22 crossing, look for Firesteed Cellars on the right-hand side of the highway.

Firesteed Cellars   *map page 149, B-2*
In the early 1990s, Seattle wine merchant Howard Rossbach noted a demand for high-quality, inexpensive pinot noir. To meet it, he teamed up with Flynn Vineyards, a Rickreall winery (founded in 1984) that had more production and storage space than it needed and a well-regarded winemaker with time on his hands. Firesteed released about 7,000 cases of its first wine from the 1992 vintage, and during the past decade its output has risen to more than 50,000 cases. In 2002, Firesteed acquired Flynn Vineyards—both the winery and its 39 acres of vineyards. Firesteed produces an Oregon pinot noir, a Willamette Valley pinot noir (from Willamette Valley grapes only), and an Oregon pinot gris, as well as a barbera d'Asti made for the winery in northern Italy. *2200 West Pacific Highway; 503-623-8683. Open daily.*

■ DALLAS

West of Firesteed off Route 22 is the **Baskett Slough National Wildlife Refuge.** The most northerly of the three Willamette Valley refuges, it was created to provide a vital wintering habitat for the dusky Canada geese, who nest on Alaska's Copper River Delta and winter almost exclusively in the Willamette Valley. Besides geese, you may spot several species of ducks, herons, hawks, quail, shorebirds, woodpeckers, and songbirds here. A small number of bald eagles winter on the refuge and can often be seen harassing the ducks and the geese. *10995 Route 22; 503-623-2749.*

Return to Salem on Route 22 to begin Tour 2.

A worker boxes bottles of wine at Willamette Valley Vineyards in Turner.

■ TOUR 2: EAST OF SALEM

■ TURNER

Head south from Salem on I-5. Take Exit 248 (Sunnyside/Turner) and follow the signs to Willamette Valley Vineyards, marked by a large entrance arch.

Willamette Valley Vineyards *map page 157, A-3*
This sprawling winery complex stands atop a vine-clad ridge in the South Salem Hills, just east of I-5. The wines, made from both estate-grown and purchased grapes, were a bit unpredictable in the years following the winery's establishment in 1988. But today's vintages of pinot noir, chardonnay, Riesling, and pinot gris have found their niche among Oregon's premium wines. The views from the tasting room and terraced picnic area, enhanced by a viewing tower, sweep across hills and valleys all the way to the Cascade Mountains. *8800 Enchanted Way SE; 503-588-9463. Open daily.*

■ SILVERTON AND MOLALLA

The next winery lies northeast of Salem, near the hamlet of Marquam, about halfway to Molalla (which is its official address). To get to it, drive back into Salem on I-5 and exit at Route 213, heading east. When you reach the city of Silverton, you may want to stop at the **Oregon Garden,** which encompasses several dozen acres of plantings. Highlights include the Signature Oak, a 400-year-old native oak—22 feet 10 inches in circumference and 99 feet tall—and other oaks whose ages range from 150 to 200 years. Also on the site are a water garden, a children's garden, and the Gordon House, the only house in Oregon designed by the master architect Frank Lloyd Wright; it was moved here from Wilsonville, 26 miles to the north, in 2001. *879 West Main Street, Silverton; 503-874-8100.*

To get to Marquam Hill Vineyards, continue driving north from Silverton on Route 213 for about 8.5 miles until you reach the winery. Signs will direct you.

Marquam Hill Vineyards *map page 157, B-2*
Marquam Hill lies far to the east of other Willamette Valley wineries, in the foothills of the Cascade Mountains. The winery is surrounded by vineyards that were first planted in 1983; grape varieties include pinot noir, chardonnay, Riesling, gewürztraminer, and Müller-Thurgau. Marquam Hill's estate bottlings

(following spread) The annual grape-stomping contest at Willamette Valley Vineyards.

prove that grapes grown on the east side of the Willamette Valley can be every bit as enticing as those grown to the west. In addition to these bottlings, the winery also produces cabernet sauvignon, pinot blanc, and sparkling wines. The picnic grounds, amid a sheltering grove of trees, overlook a lake. *35803 South Highway 213, Molalla; 503-829-6677. Open daily Memorial Day–Oct.; weekends and by appointment the rest of the year.*

From Marquam Hill, turn left on Route 213 and drive north to Route 211; take it west to I-5 and head north. At Butteville, take Exit 282A and follow the signs to the Champoeg State Heritage Area; Champoeg Wine Cellars, for which you'll also see signs, is on the way, about 35 miles from Marquam Hill Vineyards.

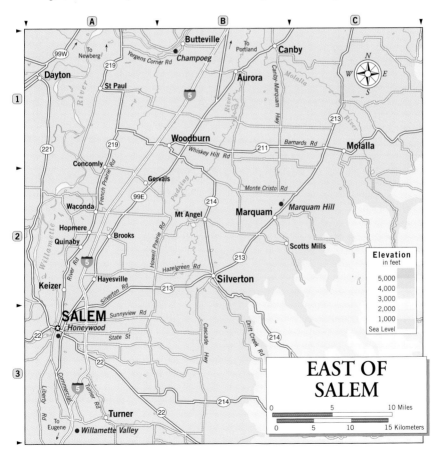

EAST OF SALEM

■ **AURORA**

Champoeg Wine Cellars *map page 157, B-1*
The Champoeg vineyard is one of the oldest wine-grape plantings in Oregon. Back in 1974, workers clearing land for the modern vineyard discovered pinot meunier grapes growing in the woods—remnants of vineyards first planted as far back as the 1840s by French-Canadian trappers who had retired from the Hudson's Bay Company. Grapes were still grown here into the 1930s; an 1880 farm report referred to neighboring Butteville as the wine capital of the Oregon Territory. The south-facing slope of the estate vineyard looks towards Champoeg, the place where Oregon settlers decided, in 1843, to give their allegiance to the United States instead of Britain. The winery produces estate-bottled pinot noir, chardonnay, Riesling, and pinot gris, as well as some Müller-Thurgau and gewürztraminer. *10375 Champoeg Road NE; 503-678-2144. Open Tues.–Sun. Closed Jan.*

From Champoeg Wine Cellars, turn right and continue past Champoeg State Heritage Area to Route 219. Turning left will take you back to Salem. Turning right will take you across the Willamette River to Newberg and the Yamhill County wine country.

Pinot noir grapes at Secret House Vineyards Winery, west of Eugene.

SOUTHERN
WILLAMETTE VALLEY

NEAR EUGENE, AS THE COAST RANGE merges into the Western Cascades, the Willamette Valley narrows and turns hilly. Gentle slopes rise from deep creek and river valleys to a series of rounded ridges. Though these hills were among the first in Oregon to be settled by the mid-19th-century pioneers—Jesse Applegate established his farm near Yoncalla in 1849—the oldest winery here, Silvan Ridge/Hinman Vineyards, dates back only to 1979. But that brief time span is no reflection on the quality of the vines and wines. Once vintners recognized how marvelous these hills were for the growing of grapes, they came to stay. So far, though, the southern Willamette Valley has many more vineyards than wineries—its grapes are eagerly sought out by wineries from other parts of the valley.

The valley is at its flattest north of Eugene, because it was here that the giant lakes formed by the huge Spokane Floods deposited hundreds—in places thousands—of feet of clays and loamy silts on top of the bedrock. (In calm lakes, sand and silt tend to settle on the bottom in smooth sheets.) The hills that are here are gentle, partly because the rocks that make up their core were formed from easily eroded mud and sandstone long ago laid down on the ocean floor, then scraped off and mounded as the North American continent began to crunch over the oceanic Farallon Plate. This process continues today, and the light soils derived from sedimentary deposits make for perfect grapevine drainage.

It's hotter here in summer and colder and snowier in winter than in the upper Willamette Valley, where marine air pouring in through the Columbia River–Oregon City gap softens the climate. However, most of the local vineyards and wineries are off to the west, along or near the Territorial Highway, where they benefit from the cooling breezes wafting in from the Pacific Ocean through the Siuslaw River Valley.

Eugene is the metropolis of southern Oregon, with the University of Oregon campus, a world-class performing arts center, and excellent hotels and restaurants. The **KoHo Bistro** (2101 Bailey Hill Road; 541-681-9335) serves elegant, beautifully presented food that changes seasonally. The dishes at **Marché** (296 East Fifth Avenue; 541-342-3612) are prepared with great élan in an open kitchen; the extensive list of Oregon wines includes some hard-to-find ones. At **Cafe Soriah** (384 West 13th Avenue; 541-342-4410), another excellent list, heavy on both Italian and Oregon wines (making it possible to compare the two), complements a menu of Mediterranean comfort food.

Bins of freshly harvested chardonnay grapes at Tyee Wine Cellars.

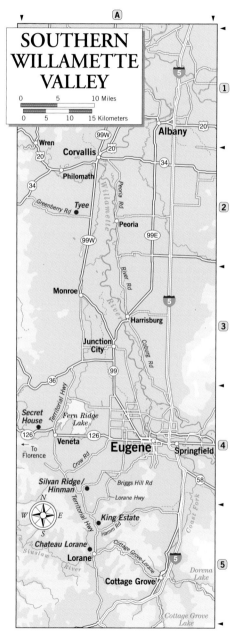

SOUTHERN WILLAMETTE VALLEY

0   5   10 Miles

0   5   10   15 Kilometers

Wren
Corvallis
Philomath
Greenberry Rd   Tyee
Monroe
Secret House
Fern Ridge Lake
Veneta
Silvan Ridge/ Hinman
Chateau Lorane
Lorane

Albany
Peoria
Harrisburg
Junction City
Eugene   Springfield
Briggs Hill Rd
Lorane Hwy
King Estate
Dorena Lake
Cottage Grove
Cottage Grove Lake

■ LOOP DRIVE FROM EUGENE

You can visit the wineries in the Southern Willamette Valley on an easy loop drive from Eugene. Head south on I-5 to Cottage Grove. Take the Cottage Grove–Lorane Road Exit (Exit 174) to Lorane and head north on the Territorial Highway and Route 99W. Return east on U.S. 20 to Albany and then south on I-5 back to Eugene.

About 22 miles south of Eugene you'll pass through **Cottage Grove,** famous for its covered bridges, all a few minutes' drive from the small downtown. On the Coast Fork of the Willamette River, Cottage Grove is a woodsy retreat with two nearby lakes, Dorena and Cottage Grove, where you can picnic, boat, fish, swim, or camp; Dorena is also popular with windsurfers.

The Siuslaw Valley is separated from Cottage Grove and the upper Willamette Valley by a ridge of low hills to its east and is hemmed in by the southern spurs of the Coast Range to its northwest. A drive through the valley is splendidly scenic; the roads wind through beautiful countryside in which verdant riparian woods alternate with lush woodlands, meadows, and rolling hills.

Oak and Douglas fir can be found all over the Southern Willamette Valley.

■ LORANE

To drive from Cottage Grove to the rural Siuslaw Valley village of Lorane, take the Cottage Grove–Lorane Road west, crossing the Territorial Highway, to Siuslaw River Road. Look for signs to Chateau Lorane (on the right). Two retail stores sit along Territorial Road, the main route through town, but the old part of town, which contains some picturesque old buildings, rises high above the highway.

Chateau Lorane *map page 164, A-5*

Chateau Lorane deserves to be better known, both for its setting and its wines. The owners, Linde and Sharon Kester, planted the 30-acre vineyard in 1984, on a wooded hillside in the upper Siuslaw River Valley west of Lorane, and opened the winery in 1992. They produce estate-grown pinot noir, chardonnay, Riesling, sauvignon blanc, and gewürztraminer. They also make wines from grapes bought from other growers—including such uncommon varieties as viognier, mélon de bourgogne, durif (more commonly known as petite sirah), and pinot meunier—as well as such enological oddities as aurora, flora, Maréchal Foch, baco noir, and cascade. Tall firs shade the picnic area, which overlooks a 24-acre lake. *27415 Siuslaw River Road; 541-942-8028. Open daily June–Sept.; weekends the rest of the year.*

■ EUGENE

After visiting Chateau Lorane, return to town and head north on the Territorial Highway. After about 4 miles, look for signs directing you to King Estate Winery.

King Estate Winery *map page 164, A-5*

It's hard to miss this imposing establishment, which rises above vineyard-clad slopes west of the highway like a turreted castle designed by a Hollywood producer. But King Estate Winery is more than a mere facade; it's solid through and through, down to the gothic vaults of the aging cellars (which double as banquet halls). Its wines—pinot noir, pinot gris, and chardonnay—are also solid: carefully made, with a special snap that may come from the microclimate and *terroir* of the hillside vineyards. Besides growing grapes for its winepress, King Estate has been instrumental in experimenting with different clones and in growing vines for other wineries at Lorane Grapevines, its nursery and vine-grafting facility—and there's nothing faux-antique about its state-of-the-art wine-making equipment. *80854 Territorial Highway; 541-942-9874. Open daily May–Oct., weekends Nov.–Apr.*

The hilltop King Estate Winery, hovering above the vineyards. (right) The annual Memorial Day celebration at Chateau Lorane.

About 6.25 miles farther north on the Territorial Highway, you'll see signs for Silvan Ridge/Hinman Vineyards.

Silvan Ridge/Hinman Vineyards *map page 164, A-4*

Established in 1979, Hinman Vineyards gained early praise, but somehow things fell apart in the 1980s, and the winery bumped along a very rough track for a while. Now, under new ownership, it's flying high, and the wines—especially the pinot noir, pinot gris, and chardonnay released under the winery's Silvan Ridge Reserve label—rank among the state's best. The winery also produces several wines under its Hinman Vineyards label, including a spry early muscat semi-sparkling wine that's perfect for a summer afternoon, an early muscat huxelrebe, and a botrytis cluster-select late-harvest Riesling. But it's the pinot noir, pinot gris, and chardonnay that will keep you coming back. The winery itself is a delight. Tucked beneath a piney ridge, the tasting room and shaded picnic area overlook a broad tree- and-vine-clad valley where hawks soar over the vineyards. You can linger here, or buy some wine and head for the beach at Florence—it's only an hour away via Route 126. The winery has occasional sales at incredible prices, announced on its Web site. *27012 Briggs Hill Road; 541-345-1945. Open daily.*

■ **VENETA**

Return to the Territorial Highway and turn left (west) on Route 126 heading toward Florence. After about 2 miles, look for signs directing you to Secret House Vineyards.

Secret House Vineyards *map page 164, A-4*

Another family-owned winery that deserves greater fame, Secret House nestles in the woods just north of busy Route 126. But as you walk the grounds or pause in the small garden, the winery seems to occupy a serene world all its own. The tranquility extends indoors to the tasting room, where fine Asian art—one of the owners is a former importer—is on display. Secret House is known for its pinot noir and chardonnay, but it also makes a crisp dry Riesling, a fruity late-harvest Riesling, and even a little *méthode champenoise* sparkling wine. Throughout the summer the winery sponsors music concerts. The most popular of these, the Wine & Blues Festival, takes place on the second weekend in August. *88324 Vineyard Lane; 541-935-3774. Open daily.*

Michael McNeill, the winemaker at Hinman Vineyards.

■ CORVALLIS

Tyee Wine Cellars, our final Southern Willamette Valley winery, is 45 miles from Secret House, a 75-minute drive. To get there, return on Route 126 to the Territorial Highway, turn left, and continue north as the highway merges into Route 99. Then keep heading north until you reach the very visible Greenberry store. Turn left, and after 2 miles look for signs directing you to the winery.

(To come to Tyee on another day, take I-5 to Albany, then U.S. 20 west to Route 99W south. After 18 miles—and after passing through the heart of Corvallis—turn right at the Greenberry store. After 2 miles, look for signs directing you to the winery.)

Tyee Wine Cellars *map page 164, A-2*
This winery, established in 1985, has been taking up an ever-increasing portion of the Buchanan Family Century Farm, established exactly a century earlier. The vineyards, planted on a former racetrack, produce first-rate pinot noir, chardonnay, pinot gris, pinot blanc, and gewürztraminer. Tyee also buys grapes

. . . and chardonnay on the vine at Tyee.

from other regional vineyards. Co-owner Barney Watson, who does enological research at Oregon State University, crafts his wines in styles reminiscent of the wines of Alsace. That's probably why the gewürztraminer and the pinot gris are Tyee's most exciting wines, but this doesn't mean the other wines aren't excellent too. Ancient Oregon oaks shade the picnic area, and a surprisingly large section of the land has never been farmed—it's as pristine as it was centuries ago. The 1.5-mile-long Beaver Pond Loop Trail winds through about 450 acres of virgin meadows, marshes, and woodlands. And, yes, you'll most likely get to see a beaver splash his tail at you. *26335 Greenberry Road; 541-753-8754. Open weekends Apr.–Dec.; other times by appointment.*

Philippe Girardet, of Girardet Wine Cellars & Vineyard in the Umpqua Valley.

UMPQUA VALLEY

UNLIKE THE OTHER WINE VALLEYS of the Pacific Northwest, the Umpqua Valley is not an open bowl but rather a maze of low, wooded hills and lush, secluded valleys—hence its popular designation as the Hundred Valleys of the Umpqua. Even in the summer heat, the hills and lush valleys benefit from the cool breezes blowing in from the Pacific Ocean. Although the valleys can warm up quickly on sunny days, as the heat increases the air rises, pulling the cool Pacific air up the canyon of the Umpqua River, as well as up the Coquille and Coos Rivers and over the low divides separating those rivers from the valley of the South Umpqua. This is the kind of weather the naturalist David Douglas encountered as he was passing through the region on October 8, 1826: "Morning cool and pleasant; day clear and warm. Thermometer in the shade 82 degrees . . . wind westerly." The summer is hot here, but not unpleasantly so. The sunny days infuse grapes with sugars and flavors; the cool evening air preserves their acids and their more intangible flavor elements—climate-wise, a perfect combination for making great wines.

Though viticulture in the Umpqua Valley doesn't rival the Willamette Valley's industry, wine grapes have been grown here for more than a hundred years. The Luelling brothers, who carried fruit trees and vines in soil-filled wagons across the Great Plains in 1847, may have brought the earliest grapes planted in the Umpqua Valley. By 1883, A.G. Walling could write in *History of Southern Oregon,* "As a fruit region, the Umpqua Valley shares with the Rogue River region the honor of producing the finest quality and greatest abundance of Oregon fruit. . . . Apples, pears, plums, cherries, peaches, apricots and grapes grow in profusion." Local viticulture got a boost that same decade when Edward and John Pessl, who had worked for Napa Valley wineries, came north and planted zinfandel, Riesling, and sauvignon vines. Adam Doerner, a German immigrant, opened his winery in 1888, in Cleveland, near Roseburg. His cuttings too came from California—zinfandel from the Napa Valley's Beringer Brothers, for whom he had worked.

In the 1960s and 1970s, most of the Pacific Northwest's pioneering vintners followed this pattern, migrating north from California in search of cool vineyards in which to grow premium grapes, and bringing with them cuttings from California vines. When Richard Sommer moved north from California to establish the HillCrest Vineyard, jump-starting Oregon's modern wine industry, the Doerner Winery was still going strong, having survived Prohibition by selling grapes to home winemakers. (It closed in 1965.) Old vines survive throughout the Umpqua Valley, many of them now used by recently established wineries.

Magnificent Toketee Falls, in the Umpqua National Forest east of Roseburg.

Sommer's story goes back to 1957, when he decided that the growing conditions in California's premium vineyards were too hot. So he set out to find a more European climate, where grapes could ripen during cool fall weather and develop an optimum balance of sugar, acid, and other flavors. He searched from northern California to southern British Columbia and finally found his ideal location in the Coast Range foothills of the Umpqua Valley. He discovered the old Doerner Winery, near Melrose, and the wine he made from its grapes proved more flavorful than wines from farther south. In 1961, Sommer planted 5 acres to grapes in the hills west of Melrose. He picked his first grapes in 1963 and tasted his first wine from them in 1964; its balance, flavor, and aroma confirmed his intuition. Over time he planted more grapes and perfected his wine-making skills; now both his vineyard and his technique have reached maturity. Other winemakers followed Sommer's lead, and the rest is Oregon history.

But not quite Umpqua Valley history. There ought to be many more wineries in the Umpqua Valley itself, the local winemakers grumble. The reason there aren't is all too clear: wineries need the support of locals as well as visitors. Unlike the northern Willamette Valley, which is an easy drive from Portland (and major investors want wineries within easy reach of home), the Umpqua Valley is far from the state's metropolitan centers. Slowly but steadily, however, the situation is changing. The new millennium has brought several excellent new wineries and new visitors along with them. And the residents are gradually waking up to the promise of wine.

Roseburg, a former lumber and cattle town, is a good base from which to explore the region, and there's much to explore besides vineyards and wineries. Roseburg's largely 19th-century business district, which slopes up a low hill above the turbulent waters of the South Umpqua River, maintains its small-town feel. The narrow, tree-shaded streets are dotted with galleries, cafes, and bookstores; large murals depict the original uses of some of the buildings. Most of the local wineries don't open before late morning, so this is a pleasant place to start your day.

Be sure to admire the majestic American elm tree next to the courthouse. More than a century old, some 70 feet high, and with a spread of more than 100 feet, this so-called Oregon Heritage Tree is truly awesome. You might also want to visit the **Douglas County Museum** (123 Museum Drive; 541-957-7007), just south of town, which you reach by taking I-5's Exit 123. It has splendid displays on local history and natural history, a grand collection of local artifacts, an excellent small bookstore, and a very helpful volunteer staff. The museum is currently assembling materials to document the history of vineyards and wineries in the Umpqua Valley.

On Route 138 about 18 miles northeast of Roseburg are the Narrows, where the Molalla, a band of the Umpqua Indians, speared and netted salmon and steelhead in a steep-walled canyon. This part of the North Umpqua River is now a popular fly-fishing spot. Farther east, in the Cascade Mountains, trails beckon hikers; so does pristine Diamond Lake, the source of the North Umpqua River, in the High Cascades. (The South Umpqua and Rogue begin in the mountains just a few miles to the south, near Crater Lake.)

But for an increasing number of visitors, the wineries of the Umpqua Valley, and the scenic drives connecting them, have become the main attraction. This is a laid-back region, and you'll find a sincere friendliness in the tasting rooms. The wineries fall into two geographic groups: those in the valleys of the South Umpqua and the Umpqua near Roseburg; and another couple downstream, on the south-facing slopes above the Umpqua, 38 miles (not quite an hour) north of Roseburg in the small river town of Elkton. It's possible to cover both regions in one day.

(following pages) Wine flows at Roseburg's Land of the Umpqua Wine Festival.

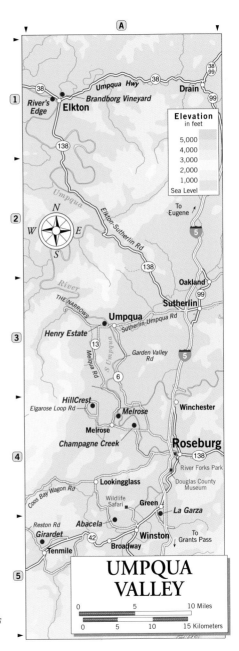

■ ROSEBURG AREA

If you think of Oregonians as staid folks dressed in Gore-Tex and hiding their webbed feet in oversized Nike sloggers, you'll enjoy the Italian liveliness that prevails at **Dino's Ristorante Italiano & Wine Bar,** which doubles as the tasting room for the DeNino Umpqua River Estate winery. The winemakers pride themselves on applying Italian wine-making methods to Bordeaux varietals—cabernet sauvignon, merlot, sauvignon blanc, sémillon—and a few others. The wines can be inconsistent, though, so taste before you buy. Dino's has a huge list and holds free tastings on Friday nights. *404 SE Jackson Street, Roseburg; 541-673-5383. Open Tues.–Sat.*

South of the Douglas County Museum, off I-5 at Exit 119, on the south side of Route 42, is our winery first stop, La Garza Cellars. Pay attention on Route 42, because the Winery Lane turnoff comes up unexpectedly before a highway causeway and is easy to miss. (There's a sign.) The access road is a narrow, bumpy gravel lane.

La Garza Cellars *map page 177, A-4*

La Garza has a checkered history. The winery opened in the early 1970s as Jonicole Winery, but it succumbed to economic troubles—a consequence, no doubt, of its unexciting wines—and sat empty until Donna Souza-Postles resurrected it in 1991. She has restored the vineyard, first planted in 1968, and it now produces excellent cabernet sauvignon. Other La Garza wines include merlot, chardonnay, a dry Riesling, and an off-dry white cabernet called Rosado de la Casa. In addition to the tasting room and gift shop, La Garza has a picnic area and a covered deck for visitors. A white-tablecloth dining room, the Gourmet Kitchen—considered by many the best in the region—serves lunch from Wednesday through Sunday between May and September, and dinners by appointment. The food is simple (salads, sandwiches, pastas) but first-rate. *491 Winery Lane, Roseburg; 541-679-9654. Open daily May–Sept. Call for hours Oct.–Apr.*

If the dining room at La Garza is closed, you can drive south from Roseburg to nearby Winston and enjoy a good lunch at the White Rhino Restaurant (541-679-1299). This place is inside the woodsy **Wildlife Safari,** where lions, rhinos, elk, and other wild things roam freely on 600 acres. Don't be surprised to see a giraffe feeding on native oaks right off the preserve road, unrestrained by any fences. You do not have to tour Wildlife Safari to eat at the restaurant. *Safari Road off Lookingglass Road (follow signs from I-5, Exit 119), Winston; 541-679-6761.*

Checking on the progress of aging wines at Abacela.

Winston is a picturesque town, more famous for its annual melon festival, held on the second weekend in September in Riverbend Park, than for its wineries. West of Winston on Lookingglass Road is the Abacela Vineyards and Winery, but unless you're coming from Wildlife Safari, the best way to reach it from La Garza is by taking Route 42 to Brockway Road and turning left onto Lookingglass Road.

Abacela Vineyards and Winery *map page 177, A-5*

Little Abacela makes big, deeply colored reds, with intense varietal character and ample fruit, tannin, and big body, allowing them to age well. The winery has limited production and very limited distribution, but its first-rate wines make a special trip well worth the effort. Here and on nearby rocky slopes thrive such relatively uncommon-to-Oregon grapes as tempranillo, syrah, malbec, grenache, albariño, and dolcetto, matched to local microclimates. Some enophiles believe that tempranillo, the classic Spanish grape, will soon occupy a place in the Northwest wine pantheon; if Abacela's incredible 2000 Tempranillo Reserve is a representative sample, they're on the money. The grapes at Abacela are picked at their peak of ripeness and processed gently in a gravity-flow winery. After the wines have finished fermenting, they're aged underground in small oak casks for several years. The ancient muzzle-loading cannon that overlooks the vineyard from the edge of the parking area is not perched there to fight off neo-Prohibitionists. *12500 Lookingglass Road, Roseburg; 541-679-6642. Open daily.*

Head west for about 11 miles on Route 42, then right on Reston Road, to reach Girardet Wine Cellars. (If you're coming from I-5, take Exit 119 south to Winston; travel west on Route 42 and turn right on Reston Road.)

Girardet Wine Cellars & Vineyard   *map page 177, A-5*

Girardet's winery building rises above its vineyards in a beautiful setting. Some enophiles find the winery's approach a bit puzzling, though. It's in a prime region for growing vinifera (Old World) wines, and though Philippe Girardet, the Swiss-born winemaker and owner, makes excellent pinot noir, chardonnay, and cabernet sauvignon, he also turns out wines from such French-American hybrids as baco noir and Maréchal Foch—grapes normally grown only in climes where the noble vinifera doesn't thrive. But these unusual wines have won him a following.

(above) A crest on the tasting room wall at Girardet Wine Cellars and Vineyard.
(following spread) River of thrills: whitewater rafting on the North Umpqua.

The winery offers visitors not only a picnic area but also a picnic pergola—a god-send on a hot southern Oregon day. *895 Reston Road, Roseburg; 541-679-7252. Open daily.*

From Girardet, turn right onto Reston Road and continue north about 3.25 miles to the Coos Bay Wagon Road. Turn right and follow this road for about 4.75 miles. Turn left onto Fluorine Valley Road, and continue along this road, which winds about through some very scenic backcountry, for about 7 miles to Melrose Road. Turn left onto Melrose; after a little less than half a mile, turn left again onto Doerner Road, then after about 1.5 miles turn right onto Elgarose Loop Road. Follow the signs to HillCrest Vineyard; it's another 1.25 miles.

Elgarose Loop Road winds through woods and meadows, with hawks circling overhead, birds singing in the thickets, deer browsing by wayside, and an occasional wild tom turkey strutting his stuff. Turkeys, by the way, are not native to southern Oregon; they were introduced as game birds and have adapted very well to the local oak woods. (If you're coming from I-5, take Exit 125 and head west on Garden Valley Road not quite 2 miles to Melrose Road; turn slightly to the left onto Melrose and, after 3 miles, slightly to the right onto Doerner Road. Continue, as above, to Elgarose Loop Road and HillCrest.)

HillCrest Vineyard *map page 177, A-4*

The oldest continuously operating vinifera winery in Oregon, HillCrest, founded in 1961 by Richard Sommer, is the quintessential Oregon winery, its well-weathered barnlike building set amid pines and vines that are almost painfully scenic. The view from the winery porch sweeps across the rugged country to the north, with a prospect of 1,629-foot-high Woodruff Mountain, 2,450-foot-high Tyee Mountain, the Umpqua River, and, on the left, the HillCrest No. 2 vineyard, where Riesling and cabernet sauvignon vines grow. (Although HillCrest produces many different wines, it specializes in late-harvest Riesling and complex bottle-aged cabernet sauvignon.) The winery is now run by Sommer's understudy, Dyson DeMara, along with his wife and children. *240 Vineyard Lane, Roseburg; 541-673-3709. Open daily.*

From HillCrest, return to Doerner Road and turn left (east) onto it. Veer left when you get to Melrose Road and make a left turn on Busenbark Lane. (If you're coming from downtown Roseburg, take I-5 to Exit 125 and head west on Garden Valley Boulevard for 2 miles, turning left on Melrose Road and, after another mile, right onto Busenbark.)

Champagne Creek Cellars *map page 177, A-4*

In 1978, Frank Guido began making red table wine under the Di Martini label in a renovated 1878 hay barn adjacent to the Guido ranch. In 1982, he joined forces with a grapegrower and produced wine under a new Garden Valley Winery label, but the partnership didn't last. In 1987, he created Callahan Ridge Winery on the same site. It lasted until 2001, when David and Janiece Brown took over the property and renamed it Champagne Creek Cellars—though the actual Champagne Creek is not here but to the east, near the South Umpqua. Champagne Creek makes wines from grapes grown in the Umpqua Valley, including some from the historic farm where Adam Doerner first planted zinfandel in the late 1800s. It currently produces very reasonably priced (mostly less than $10 a bottle) pinot gris, gewürztraminer, Riesling, chardonnay, pinot noir, gamay noir, cabernet sauvignon, and rosé—but no Champagne. There's a nice picnic area. *340 Busenbark Lane, Roseburg; 541-673-7901. Open daily.*

During spring and fall, produce stands along the back roads sell fresh fruits and vegetables. A picnic area at **River Forks Park** (River Forks Park Road; 541-673-6935), at the confluence of the North and South Umpqua Rivers, marks the spot where pioneers on the Applegate Trail forded the river in the mid-19th century. To get there from Champagne Creek Cellars, return to Melrose Road and turn left (east); after about a mile and a quarter, turn left onto Garden Valley Road and follow it for about 2.5 miles, then turn left again onto Old Garden Valley Road. After a little more than half a mile, turn sharply left onto River Forks Park Road.

If you're not going to the park, backtrack from Champagne Creek Cellars to Melrose Road, drive west to Melqua Road, and turn right (north). It's a half-mile drive from this intersection to Melrose Vineyards.

Melrose Vineyards *map page 177, A-4*

The extensive grapevine plantings at Melrose Vineyards spread out on a site once occupied by a 19th-century French pioneer settlement. Until a few years ago, Melrose was just a grower, supplying grapes to many of Oregon's premium wineries. Although it still sells its grapes, Melrose now makes its own wine as well, in a restored century-old barn that also contains a tasting room. In just a couple of years of operation, the winery has become recognized for its estate pinot noir, blended from the juice of several different pinot noir clones that it grows. The winery grounds are a good place for a picnic. *885 Melqua Road, Roseburg; 541-672-6080. Open daily.*

A building mural in Roseburg by Susan Applegate depicts a scene along the Applegate Trail.

Continue driving north, over the hills, on Melqua Road. After about 8 miles, turn right onto the Hubbard Creek Road, which will take you in about half a mile to the Henry Estate Winery.

If you're coming from I-5, take Exit 136 at Sutherlin. Turn left (west), and take Route 128 for about a quarter of a mile before bearing left into Fort McKay Road. Follow this road west for about 7.5 miles; it changes its name en route, first to Sutherlin Umpqua Road and then to Hubbard Creek Road. The winery is on the right, just after you after you cross the Umpqua River.

Henry Estate Winery *map page 177, A-3*

The scent of roses wafts through the air at the Henry Estate Winery, which looks more like a lodge than a winery. The operation took shape when Scott Henry, an aeronautical engineer, came home to the family farm in 1972 and planted vineyards on land the family had owned for 75 years. But the vineyards, spread across scenic bottomlands near the Umpqua River, had a problem: their soils were *too* fertile to make good wine. To deal with it, Henry came up with a new trellising system that gives the vines the stress they need to produce better

grapes. (The system is now used in many parts of the world.) Henry Estate Winery produces high-quality chardonnay, pinot noir, Müller-Thurgau, cabernet sauvignon, white Riesling, and gewürztraminer; the gewürztraminer, which lacks the bitterness too often found in West Coast versions of this wine, is among the best in North America. The winery has a picnic area shaded by a grape arbor and flanked by pretty flower gardens. It holds its Henry Goes Wine festival (with wine, food, music, carriage rides, and family activities) on the third Saturday in August. *687 Hubbard Creek Road, Umpqua; 541-459-5120. Open daily.*

If you're continuing on from Henry Estate Winery, to Elkton, continue east on Hubbard Creek Road to Sutherlin Umpqua Road, which becomes Fort McKay Road. After a little less than 4 miles, make a left on Cole Road. After 0.75 miles, turn right on Wilcox Road, staying on it for a little more than a mile until you hit Route 138. Head north (left) until you get to Elkton, 23 miles farther along. (From Roseburg, travel north on I-5 to Exit 135, and take Route 138 north.)

■ ELKTON

Elkton is a sleepy river town with faded facades of business buildings lining its main street, but long ago this was an important place. In the mid-1830s, the Hudson's Bay Company set up its Fort Umpqua trading post across the river from the modern-day town. Elkton became the county seat of Umpqua County in 1851, but lost the title after just 11 years, when Umpqua County merged into Douglas County. By late in the 19th century, Elkton had gristmills and lumber mills, some of which were destroyed by the periodic Umpqua River floods. Elkton began its long sleep after the railroads bypassed the town—a slumber from which it is now slowly emerging.

Brandborg Vineyard and Winery   *map page 177, A-1*
Brandborg Cellars moved north from Richmond, California, in the spring of 2001 because Terry and Sue Brandborg were looking for perfect pinot noir land. Their newly planted vineyard stretches over 145 acres in the coastal hills high above the Umpqua Valley, on well-drained, south-facing slopes. The Brandborgs are also planning to experiment with other Umpqua Valley–suited varieties; for

Two scenes from the Henry Goes Wine festival, the Henry Estate Winery's annual blowout, which includes plenty to eat, including lamb kebabs with Umpqua Valley mushrooms.

their first Oregon vintage, in addition to pinot noir they purchased Riesling, gewürztraminer, pinot gris, cabernet franc, and syrah grapes. *345 First Street; 541-584-2870. Open daily Memorial Day–Labor Day; weekends and by appointment Oct.–Dec. and Mar.–May. Closed Jan.–Feb.*

From Brandborg, take First Street south across Route 38 and turn right onto River Drive; follow this road west for about a mile to River's Edge Winery, which will be on your right just before the junction of River Drive and Route 38.

River's Edge Winery   *map page 177, A-1*

River's Edge occupies a spartan building, but don't let that put you off—the quality here lies in the pinot noir, pinot noir reserve, and gewürztraminer, all produced from grapes grown in two estate vineyards. The winery uses low-tech, labor-intensive methods to make its wines: they're all fermented in small batches and aged in barrels. The tasting room overlooks the Umpqua River. *1395 River Drive; 541-584-2357. Open daily Memorial Day weekend–Labor Day; Wed.–Sun. Sept.–Nov. Closed Dec.–Memorial Day weekend.*

Cool-climate grapes at the Bear Creek Winery, in the Illinois River Valley.

ROGUE RIVER VALLEY

A picture-postcard day on the Applegate River.

THE ROGUE RIVER'S 215-MILE COURSE to the sea begins in the High Cascades near Crater Lake—only a few miles from the sources of the North and South Umpqua Rivers—and ends at Gold Beach on the coast. Its twisted and precipitous path cuts through the rugged Cascade and Siskiyou Mountains, with only a few valleys level enough to allow for agriculture and settlements. The largest and most populous, the Bear Creek Valley, runs from Ashland north to the Rogue near Central Point and includes the towns of Talent and Medford; it has long been famous for its cheeses, as well as for pears and other tree fruits, and it has recently become famous for its wines, especially Bordeaux-style reds. The pastoral Applegate River Valley, a separate appellation within the larger Rogue River Valley AVA, runs south from Grants Pass; some of Oregon's earliest vineyards were planted here, in the 1850s, and in the last decades of the 20th century it again became a nexus of wine production. The upper Illinois River Valley, southwest of Grants Pass near Cave Junction, was mainly a center of cattle ranching, logging, and mining until recently, when it became better known for the high quality of its wines.

The Siskiyou Mountains, a northeastern range of the Klamath Mountains, spread across this region, giving it the most convoluted landscape in Oregon—

with steep cliffs, narrow canyons, whitewater rivers, and serene, bucolic valleys. It gets quite hot here in the summer. The vegetation is more akin to California's than to the plant communities of the Pacific Northwest. Where sere local hillsides are not covered with manzanita and ceanothus chaparral, they're spiked with canyon live oak, California black oak, ponderosa pine, bristlecone pine, and sugar pine. California laurel (or Oregon myrtle, as it's known here) and golden chinquapin mingle with willows and cottonwoods in the draws.

This chapter is divided into tours through the three major valleys, beginning in the Bear Creek Valley at Ashland and heading up I-5 north to Medford; continuing to Jacksonville and Grants Pass in the Applegate River Valley; then turning south on U.S. 199 for the trip to Cave Junction and the Illinois River Valley. We'll hit a final winery in Gold Hill, on the way back to Ashland. You can cover all three valleys in a day; or, alternatively, you can save the Illinois Valley wineries near Cave Junction for another day and combine a visit to them with a trip to the Oregon Caves.

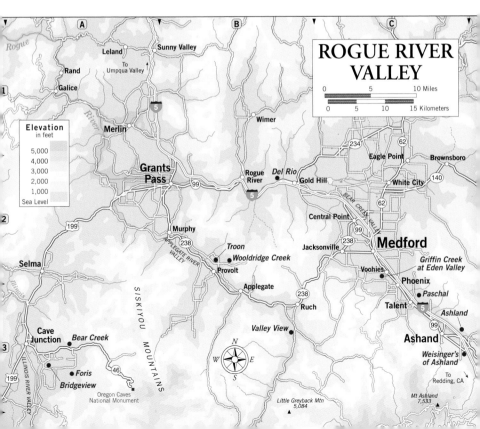

■ BEAR CREEK VALLEY

Bear Creek runs from the slopes just below Siskiyou Summit (the most important mountain pass on I-5), northwest through a wide grassy valley bordered by rolling hills, to the Rogue River north of Central Point. Along its lower course, below Ashland, it marks the boundary between two major mountain systems, the Siskiyous and the Cascades. To the west, it's overlooked by 7,533-foot-high Mount Ashland and the sharp ridges of the Siskiyous; to the east, by the 9,495-foot-high snowy volcanic cone of Mount McLoughlin and the western Cascades. Tucked amid such vertical companions, the Bear Creek Valley itself lies at a higher altitude than other Oregon wine regions. Vineyards rise from an elevation of about 1,100 feet above sea level, near Gold Hill, to about 2,000 feet, east of Ashland. Because the valley is hemmed in by mountain ranges that protect it from the influx of cool marine air, it is Oregon's warmest growing region, well suited to the ripening of such warm-climate grape varieties as merlot, cabernet sauvignon, cabernet franc, sauvignon blanc, and syrah; some of Oregon's richest and most complex Bordeaux-style wines are grown in Bear Creek Valley vineyards. But chardonnay and pinot gris also do surprisingly well here.

■ ASHLAND

Our tour begins in Ashland, the best-known town in the region because of the world-class Oregon Shakespeare Festival, which lasts from late winter into the fall. Ashland's lively tourist scene has provided the impetus for some fine restaurants.

Chateaulin (50 East Main Street; 541-482-2264)—half a city block from the theaters—serves excellent French dinners in a cozy bistro setting. Other fine restaurants in town include the **Ashland Creek Bar & Grill** (92 North Main Street; 541-482-4131); **Il Giardino** (5 Granite Street; 541-488-0816); **Macaroni's Ristorante** (58 East Main Street; 541-488-3359); and **Monet Restaurant and Garden** (36 South Second Street; 541-482-1339). The most elegant place to stay here is the **Ashland Springs Hotel** (212 East Main Street; 541-488-1700).

Mount Ashland, to the south, is known for its skiing, for its wildflower meadows (in blossom, depending on the year, between June and August), and for its wonderful views north into Oregon and south into California.

To get to Weisinger's, our first winery stop, drive south Route 99 for 1.5 miles to Green Springs Highway/Route 66 and turn left (east). After 6 miles, turn right on Old Siskiyou Highway and continue for 2.5 miles to the winery.

Weisinger's of Ashland, and a fine view of the Bear Creek Valley.

Weisinger's of Ashland *map page 193, C-3*

This small family winery, which John Weisinger opened in 1989 (his son Eric is now the winemaker), turns out limited-production wines from grapes grown in the Rogue and Applegate Valleys. Current offerings include chardonnay, dry gewürztraminer, cabernet sauvignon, and merlot. But Weisinger's believes, almost aggressively, that the best wines are made from grapes that have been blended together, and it's best known for its proprietary red-wine blends: Mescolare (a blend of pinot noir, cabernet sauvignon, and nebbiolo) and Petite Pompadour (a classic Bordeaux blend of merlot, cabernet sauvignon, cabernet franc, and malbec). Visitors may picnic on the deck overlooking the valley—a great place for watching sunsets if you happen to be here late in the day. *3150 Siskiyou Boulevard; 541-488-5989. Open daily May–Sept.; Wed.–Sun. Oct.–Apr.*

After leaving Weisinger's, turn north and return to the junction of Old Siskiyou Highway and Route 99. Continue north for about three quarters of a mile to Main Street and turn right at the Y in the road. Continue north for a little less than half a mile to the next winery.

Ashland Vineyards & Winery *map page 193, C-3*

When this family-owned winery arrived on the scene in 1987, there were few grapevines in southern Oregon. The winery not only remedied that situation but also applied and obtained approval for the Rogue Valley AVA—which in turn helped attract other winemakers to the region by alerting them to the fact that local climates and soils were suitable for producing premium wines. The 120-acre estate vineyard is organic—the winegrower uses no pesticides or herbicides on the grapes. Bottlings include cabernet franc, chardonnay, sauvignon blanc, pinot gris, an esteemed merlot, a cabernet sauvignon–merlot blend, and a cabernet sauvignon–cabernet franc blend the winery bills as the Bordeaux of Oregon. *2775 East Main Street; 541-488-0088. Open daily except Mon.*

■ TALENT

From Ashland Vineyards and Winery, drive south, turning right (west) onto Route 66; take Exit 14 to drive north on I-5. Drive north on I-5 the 7 miles to Talent, and take Exit 21. Turn right onto Valley View Road (crossing the freeway), then right onto Route 99 and almost immediately turn onto Suncrest Road. Follow Suncrest (and the signs) to Paschal Winery (about a mile up the hill; turn right at the Y).

Talent, by the way, has one of the region's best restaurants, an incongruously plain place named **New Sammy's Cowboy Bistro** (2210 Pacific Highway; 541-535-2779), which also has the region's best wine list. Chef Charlene Rollins's food might be described as simple but elegant country cookery: fresh seasonal ingredients and rich, complex flavors.

Paschal Winery *map page 193, C-3*

This small winery gained renown for its Bordeaux-style reds—cabernet sauvignon, merlot, and its Quartet blend of cabernet franc, cabernet sauvignon, merlot, and malbec—and for small quantities of syrah, pinot gris, pinot blanc, and pinot noir. But Joe Dobbes, formerly of Willamette Valley Vineyards and Torii Mor, took over in 2002 and switched Paschal to Italian varietals such as sangiovese and dolcetto (he also has plans for a Super Tuscan blend), purchasing his grapes from southern Oregon vineyards. Paschal will continue to make cabernet sauvignon and merlot but will discontinue the other Bordeaux varieties. The winery's beautiful hilltop tasting room has views of the Bear Creek Valley and the Siskiyou and southern Cascade Mountains. *1122 Suncrest Road; 541-535-7957. Open daily except Mon.*

■ MEDFORD AND CENTRAL POINT

From Paschal, backtrack on Suncrest Road to Route 99 and turn right, heading north. After about 5 miles, turn left onto Stage Road South and follow it for about 5.5 miles to Voorhies Road. Turn left. Griffin Creek and Eden Valley Orchards are immediately to the south.

Griffin Creek at Eden Valley Orchards *map page 193, C-2*

Eden Valley Orchards is the birthplace of southern Oregon's pear industry. Here, in 1885, the first pear trees were planted. The estate's Voorhies Mansion, framed by formal gardens, is a local landmark; its former carriage house has been turned into a wine education center and a market selling gourmet foods and wine-related objects. You can picnic in the pavilion overlooking the vineyards. Griffin Creek wines are produced from grapes grown in the Rogue River Valley by Don and Traute Moore, but instead of being vinified here they're shipped to Willamette Valley Vineyards in Turner, south of Salem, where they're fermented, bottled, and shipped back south. The emphasis is on Bordeaux and Rhône varieties, notably merlot. The tasting room at Eden Valley Orchards also pours wines from other small local wineries, including Troon Vineyard (see Grants Pass, on page 202). *2310 Voorhies Road; 541-512-9463. Open daily May–Sept.; Tues.–Sat. Oct.–Apr.*

Medford, the regional metropolis (which is on Bear Creek, not the Rogue River), is a fruit-packing town that has recently fallen victim to urban sprawl—as the local residents are painfully aware. It has many of the valley's malls, with most located, conveniently for travelers, close to I-5.

Central Point, immediately northwest of Medford along I-5, got its name in the second half of the 19th century, when it was the center of settlement in the Rogue River and Bear Creek Valleys. After the railroad arrived from California, Central Point became a shipping center for produce.

Today, Central Point is famous for Oregon Blue Vein Cheese, which you can purchase at the **Rogue Creamery.** The Creamery makes four different kinds of blue cheese, which differ in culture, fat content, flavor, and texture, but not in quality. It makes several cheddars as well. The cheese curds are great road snacks. The Creamery also sells a variety of local wines from small producers. *311 North Front Street; 541-665-1155.*

(following pages) Cabernet sauvignon grapes ripening at the Applegate River Valley's historic Valley View Winery.

■ APPLEGATE RIVER VALLEY

The Applegate brothers—Jesse, Charles, and Lindsay—opened the southern overland trail to Oregon and explored the region in 1846, giving their name both to the Applegate Trail and to the river that flows into the Rogue west of Grants Pass. It was in the valley of the Applegate River that Oregon's first winery was founded, in 1854, by the Swiss immigrant photographer Peter Britt, near the gold rush town of Jacksonville. But Britt wasn't the only farmer to plant wine grapes in southern Oregon. Alfred H. Carson planted vines above Board Shanty Creek, and in 1883, when the Oregon and California Railroad reached Grants Pass from the north, he began shipping them out by train. Carson was said to own Oregon's largest vineyard, but today no traces remain. Farther up Boot Shanty Creek, Carl F. Gentner, a German immigrant, planted a vineyard, as well as an orchard of fruit trees. John Burroughs's vineyard, planted in 1880, was said to rival Carson's by 1885, but no traces survive of it, either. Grapes, however, continued to be an integral part of Rogue River horticulture, allowing the winemakers arriving in the 1960s and 1970s to take advantage of decades of viticultural experience.

A low range of hills separates the Applegate River Valley from the Bear Creek Valley, to its east. The Applegate Valley is cooler and moister, but it's warmer and drier than the Illinois River Valley, to its west, from which it is separated by 1,500-foot-high ridges and by the 5,084-foot-high Little Greyback Mountain. The region has warm to hot summer and autumn days, cool nights, and deep, well-drained soil that contains a great deal of granite. The middle and upper valley are presently planted to merlot, cabernet sauvignon, zinfandel, and chardonnay.

■ JACKSONVILLE

Jacksonville, a town with impressive gold rush architecture, hosts the summer Britt Festivals of music and art, with classical, jazz, blues, and other concerts, as well as dance performances. The **Jacksonville Inn** (175 East California Street; 541-899-1900), in a restored building from 1863, has excellent food and a superb wine list.

Despite its mailing address, Valley View Winery lies south of Jacksonville, near the village of Ruch. To get there from Griffin Creek, go north on Voorhies Road and turn left (west) on Stage Road South. The road changes names several times; in Jacksonville it becomes California Street and merges into Route 238, the Jacksonville Highway. Take this highway south for 8 miles to Ruch, turn left on Upper Applegate Road, and follow it for about a mile to the winery.

Valley View Winery *map page 193, B-3*

Valley View takes its name from Peter Britt's 1850s enterprise on the same site. The Wisnovsky family planted its vineyards here in 1972, and released its first vintage in 1978. True to the region's strengths, recent vintages of cabernet sauvignon and other powerful reds (merlot, syrah) have rivaled California wines costing three or four times as much. The winery takes advantage of the valley's great variety of soils and microclimates to produce cabernet franc and chardonnay as well. Wines from special vintages bear the Anna Maria label, named for the family matriarch. The tasting pavilion has sweeping views of the vineyards and the Siskiyou Mountains. An alpaca ranch adjoining the property to the north is open to visitors most weekends—and if alpacas strike you as exotic, consider that they're native to the Americas, though the horses and cows grazing on nearby pastures are not. Nor are wine grapes—yet somehow they all do fine here. *1000 Upper Applegate Road; 541-899-8468. Open daily.*

Return to Route 238 and continue north along it about 30 miles, to U.S. 199 at Grants Pass.

Red-wine grapes at Valley View Winery.

■ **GRANTS PASS**

Grants Pass, at the confluence of the Rogue and Applegate Rivers, is a former lumber town slowly converting itself into a center for outdoor activities and the arts—and, like Medford, for an ever-increasing number of shopping malls. This commercial aspect translates into major traffic delays along U.S. 199, the road to the Illinois River Valley and the coast; the gaggle of traffic lights along the highway is out of sync, further slowing heavy traffic.

Restaurants worth visiting here include the **Hamilton River House** (1936 Rogue River Highway; 541-479-3938); the **River Rock Cafe** (966 SW Sixth Street; 541-479-7204); and **Wild River Brewing & Pizza Company** (595 NE E Street; 541-471-7487). Outside Grants Pass, 15 miles west of Merlin, **Morrison's Rogue River Lodge** (8500 Galice Road, Merlin; 541-476-3825), dates back to the 1940s, when it was popular with Hollywood stars. Even now you might encounter the occasional celebrity coming here to do some fly fishing or to run the Rogue's white-water rapids.

Grants Pass has two notable wineries that, unfortunately, aren't open to the public (or at least weren't at this writing; you might want to double-check to see if anything has changed). **Troon Vineyard** (1475 Kubli Road; 541-846-6562) was planted back in 1972 to cabernet sauvignon, zinfandel, and chardonnay, and some of its cabernet has been outstanding. The winemaker is Donna Devine, formerly of Siskiyou Vineyards Winery. Its wines are for sale at some local restaurants and wine shops and may be tasted at the Eden Valley Orchards tasting room (see Bear Creek Valley, on page 197) and ordered from the winery. **Wooldridge Creek Wines** (818 Slagle Creek Road; 541-846-6310), a cooperative venture between Wooldridge Creek Vineyards and two local winemakers, produces cabernet sauvignon, merlot, syrah, chardonnay, and viognier that are sold in stores and restaurants throughout Oregon. The winery is open for tastings by appointment, and its wines are available by mail order.

To get to the third of the valleys in the the Rogue River appellation, take U.S. 199 south from Grants Pass to Cave Junction, about 29 miles.

■ **ILLINOIS RIVER VALLEY**

The Illinois River, which flows from California's Klamath Mountains north into Oregon, widens from south of Cave Junction to north of Kerby, where it plunges into the steep canyons of the Klamaths. It joins the Rogue considerably farther

north, at the hamlet of Agness. The Illinois Valley, lying only about 25 miles from the Pacific Ocean, is the westernmost valley in the Rogue River Valley appellation. It's also the coolest—this is the only part of the region that benefits from the breezes coming in off the Pacific Ocean—and is planted to such cool-climate grapes as pinot noir, gewürztraminer, pinot gris, chardonnay, pinot blanc, early muscat, and gamay noir.

■ CAVE JUNCTION

Cave Junction has filling stations, fast-food restaurants, a motel or two, traffic lights, and not much else. Its single claim to fame is the fact that it straddles the junction of U.S. 199 and Route 46, the road to the **Oregon Caves,** 45 miles away. These labyrinthine caves, carved by water into limestone and marble, are one of the wonders of the West. Daily tours take visitors on a hike (not recommended for those with disabilities or heart problems) through the steep and sometimes slippery passages. The rustic, cedar-shake **Cave Chateau** (20000 Cave Highway; 541-592-3400) is a good place to stay there.

Take Route 46 east for about 5 miles from Cave Junction to reach the Bear Creek Winery.

Bear Creek Winery *map page 193, A-3*

As confusing as it may seem, Bear Creek Winery is not in the Bear Creek Valley but in the Illinois Valley. (A small stream named Bear Creek—a common name in the Northwest—flows through the property.) It occupies the site of the former Siskiyou Vineyards Winery, whose land was planted in 1969 to cabernet sauvignon, pinot noir, and gewürztraminer; additional pinot noir and pinot blanc were planted in 1999. This winery releases its prime Bordeaux varietals under the Bear Creek label, and some other wines, including pinot blanc, chardonnay, Riesling, and gewürztraminer, under the Siskiyou label. Owner and winemaker René Eichmann got his start at nearby Bridgeview winery back in 1986, and is usually on hand to discuss local vineyards and vintages with winery visitors. *6220 Caves Highway; 541-592-3977. Open daily Memorial Day–Labor Day; other times by appointment.*

Turn west from Bear Creek Winery onto Caves Highway, and after about a fifth of a mile turn left onto Holland Loop Road, following it for almost 3 miles to Althouse Road, which becomes Kendall Road. Foris Vineyards is about a fifth of a mile farther along, at the end of the narrow one-lane road.

Foris Vineyards *map page 193, A-3*

Foris is off the beaten path, tucked into cool woods surrounded by the conifer-covered Siskiyou Mountains. (*Foris* is Latin for "out of doors.") It lies just 6 miles from the Oregon-California state line, making it the Pacific Northwest's southernmost winery; it's also one of the best. Foris has experimented with Alsatian and Burgundian varieties in the varied soils of its estate vineyards, and also buys Bordeaux varieties from warmer vineyards to the east. Foris wines include pinot gris, pinot blanc, chardonnay, gewürztraminer, cabernet, merlot, cabernet franc (in blends), and a port. A few picnic tables stand scattered under the trees. This is a very relaxed, friendly place where you can get honest answers to your questions about local wines. *654 Kendall Road; 800-843-6747. Open daily.*

From Foris, backtrack north on Kendall and Althouse Roads. Turn left (west) onto Holland Loop Road and follow it for about 3.5 miles to Bridgeview.

Bridgeview Vineyard and Winery *map page 193, A-3*

Bridgeview, one of Oregon's largest wineries, sits amid acres of vineyards densely planted in the European style. Rocky river-bottom soils lend distinctive, delicious aromas and flavors to the grapes. Robert and Lelo Kerivan planted their first vines in the spring of 1980, and completed their winery in the spring of 1986; they make pinot noir, pinot gris, chardonnay, and Riesling from their own grapes, and cabernet sauvignon and merlot from grapes they buy from local vineyards. Bridgeview has indulged in some odd packaging over the years, but that has not detracted from the consistently high quality of the wines. The winery property is a welcome oasis on a summer's afternoon. Several small waterfalls connect a series of landscaped ponds where ducks, swans, and Canada geese while away the day. The tasting room and picnic area are surrounded by beautifully laid-out grounds, with stately oaks and panoramic views of the countryside. You can buy one of Bridgeview's blue moon-shaped bottles and sip a well-chilled chardonnay or Riesling as you watch the swans sail by. *4210 Holland Loop Road; 541-592-4688. Open daily.*

For the end of the tour, we'll backtrack through the Rogue River Valley on the return trip to Ashland. From Bridgeview, turn right onto Holland Loop Road and drive north 2 miles. Turn left onto Caves Highway and follow it back to Cave Junction. Turn right on U.S. 199 and drive the 30 miles north to Grants Pass, then

Workers trim the vines at Del Rio, southern Oregon's largest vineyard.

get onto I-5 there and take it south for about 12 miles to Gold Hill (Exit 43). After a fifth of a mile, turn left on Main Street; after another fifth of a mile, turn right onto Route 234/99 (the Rogue River Highway); then, after half a mile, go left on North River Road. Del Rio Vineyards is about 300 feet farther along.

■ GOLD HILL

Gold Hill is another town popular with visitors for its well-preserved gold rush architecture. It's part of the Rogue River Valley but outside the boundaries of the Bear Creek, Applegate, and Illinois River Valleys.

Del Rio Vineyards *map page 193, B-2*
Southern Oregon's largest vineyard (with more than 200,000 vines on 180 well-drained acres overlooking the Rogue River) recently became a winery as well. The vineyard's south-facing slopes ripen grapes a week or two earlier than other local vineyards, because the dry soil here collects the summer's heat and speeds the grapes' maturing. Del Rio supplies about two dozen Oregon wineries with varietal grapes (including sangiovese, nebbiolo, merlot, cabernet sauvignon, syrah, grenache, pinot noir, malbec, cabernet franc, pinot gris, chardonnay, and viognier), but it also sells its own bottlings. The 2001 vintage includes a pinot gris, a cabernet franc, and a claret (a blend of cabernet sauvignon, cabernet franc, malbec, and merlot). The tasting room occupies the Rock Point Stage Hotel, built in 1864 and partially restored to its original state. The picnic area offers views of the vineyards and the valley. *52 North River Road; 541-855-2062. Open daily.*

To return to Ashland, drive back to I-5 and head south; it's a 26-mile trip.

Racked bottles at an Oregon winery.

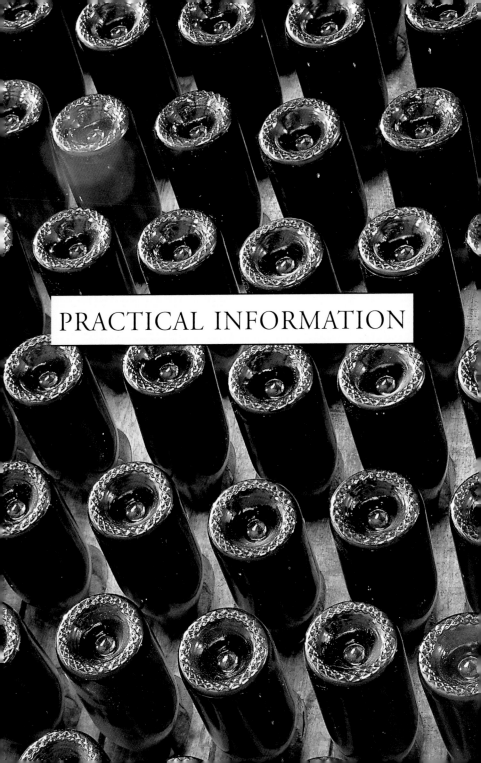

PRACTICAL INFORMATION

■ AREA CODES AND TIME ZONE

The area code in central and southern Oregon is 541; Portland and coastal Oregon use 503 and 971. The state is in the Pacific time zone.

■ METRIC CONVERSIONS

1 foot = .305 meters   1 mile = 1.6 kilometers   1 pound = .45 kilograms
Centigrade = Fahrenheit temperature minus 32, divided by 1.8

■ CLIMATE/WHEN TO GO

Oregon's Wine Country has a truly benign climate, though it's a little less so in the Rogue Valley, to the south, than it is in Portland, to the north. But even in the hot southern valleys, which can experience summer daytime temperatures of 90 to 100 degrees Fahrenheit, the nights are cool (from 50 to 55 degrees)—perfect for growing grapes. July, August, and September, the traditional travel months, are also the driest. Spring and early autumn are also fine times to visit; though the weather can be a tad unstable, spring wildflowers and fall foliage more than make up for any inconvenience. Oregon gets few visitors during late fall and winter, because the weather then can be outright rude, with weeks of steady, enervating, drizzly rains interrupted by cyclonic storms that can flood the rivers and precipitate landslides.

Two major events—the Memorial Day weekend and Thanksgiving weekend open houses, when many wineries not open at other times receive visitors—usually have good weather. Christmas and New Year's do not. In fact, the last two weeks of the old year and the first of the new can have some of the region's worst weather, with the rain and fog augmented by snow and ice—which can strike even the lowlands of the I-5 corridor between Eugene and Portland.

■ GETTING THERE AND AROUND

■ BY AIR

Portland International Airport (PDX) is the major airport in Oregon. From there service is available to the state's smaller cities. Other airports are in Eugene, Medford, Bend, Klamath Falls, and points farther east. Portland International is about 12 miles northeast of downtown Portland, about a 30 minute-drive. *7000 NE Airport Way; 503-460-4234 or 877-739-4636; www.portlandairportpdx.com.*

■ By Car

Most Oregon wineries lie a few miles off the major north-south routes traversing the western part of the state. The most important of these is I-5, which enters Oregon south of Siskiyou Summit and leaves via the Columbia River bridge north of Portland. Running west to east, I-84 follows the route of the old overland trail, connecting Oregon to the Rocky Mountain states, the Midwest, and points beyond.

U.S. 26 runs west from Portland to the coast, passing through the Washington County wine country. Route 6 and Route 210, state highways, wind through a bucolic landscape of green valleys and wooded hills on the way to Oregon's northernmost wineries. Route 47 runs south to McMinnville, and Route 240 connects the wineries of eastern Yamhill County to the western ones.

Route 99W runs from I-5 south of Portland to McMinnville and Yamhill County, then turns south to Corvallis and Eugene, passing the Eola Hills en route. This mostly two-lane highway provides a scenic alternative to I-5. Route 221 runs south from Route 99W between the Eola Hills and the Willamette Valley, facilitating access to several wineries. Route 22 heads west from Salem to Route 99W and central Willamette Valley wineries. The Territorial Highway, which splits off Route 99W at Monroe, south of Corvallis, leads to the southern Willamette Valley.

Most Umpqua Valley wineries are within easy driving distance of I-5. The northernmost, in Elkton, can be reached by taking Route 38 west and then driving to Roseburg via Route 138; the southernmost are just off Route 42, which runs west from Winston (south of Roseburg) to the coast.

The Rogue River Valley wineries can be reached from Grants Pass via U.S. 199 and Route 238 (for the Applegate Valley) or Route 46 (for the Illinois Valley), or from Medford via Route 238 and U.S. 199/Route 46. U.S. 199 continues to the coast and connects to U.S. 101 north of Crescent City, California.

■ By Train

Amtrak's route from southern California into Canada runs through Klamath Falls, Eugene, and Portland. A train from Salt Lake City terminates in Portland after passing through several towns in eastern Oregon. *800-872-7245; www.amtrak.com.*

■ By Bus

Greyhound provides service from elsewhere on the West Coast and from points east. *800-231-2222; www.greyhound.com.*

■ RESTAURANTS

Below are capsule reviews of restaurants in the Oregon Wine Country, many of which serve locally made wines. Several of the establishments are discussed in greater detail in the "Food and Wine" or regional chapters.

ENTRÉE PRICES PER PERSON

$ = less than $15   **$$** = $15–$25   **$$$** = over $25

■ PORTLAND

Heathman. One of the state's best dining rooms. *Heathman Hotel, SW Broadway at Salmon Street; 503-241-4100. Pacific Northwest.* **$$–$$$**

Jo Bar & Rotisserie. Meat, seafood, and pasta dishes from the brick oven or open rotisserie. *715 NW 23rd Avenue; 503-222-0048. Contemporary.* **$$**

Lucere. There are views of the Willamette from every table here. *RiverPlace Hotel, 1510 SW Harbor Way; 503-228-3233. Pacific Northwest/French.* **$$**

Paley's Place. A delightful bistro-style establishment in the Nob Hill area. *1204 NW 21st Avenue; 503-243-2403. Pacific Northwest/French.* **$$**

Wildwood. Chef Cory Schreiber comes from an old Oregon family. *NW 21st Avenue and Overton Street; 503-248-9663. Pacific Northwest.* **$$–$$$**

■ WILLAMETTE VALLEY

CARLTON

Caffe Bisbo. A singing cook, superb northern Italian dishes, a good wine list, and divine tiramisu. *214 West Main Street; 503-852-7248, Italian.* **$$**

DAYTON

Joel Palmer House. *The* place in the Oregon Wine Country to taste wild mushrooms. *600 Ferry Street; 503-864-2995. Pacific Northwest/Eclectic.* **$$–$$$**

DUNDEE

Dundee Bistro. The folks at Ponzi Vineyards do well by food too. *100A SW Seventh Street; 503-554-1650. Contemporary.* **$–$$**

Red Hills Provincial Dining. European cuisine served in an old-style farmhouse. *276 Highway 99W; 503-538-8224. European/Pacific Northwest.* **$$$**

Tina's. Tiny, atmospheric. Country-French dishes with a Pacific Northwest twist. *760 Highway 99W; 503-538-8880. Pacific Northwest/French.* **$$–$$$**

EUGENE
Cafe Soriah. Mediterranean comfort food is served here, with Italian and Oregon wines. *384 West Fifth Avenue; 541-342-4410. Contemporary/Eclectic.* **$$**

Excelsior Cafe. The bistro-style menu includes inventive salads. *754 East 13th Avenue; 541-342-6963. Contemporary.* **$$**

KoHo Bistro. A neighborhood bistro with seasonally changing dishes, beautifully presented. *2101 Bailey Hill Road; 541-681-9335. Contemporary.* **$$**

Marché Restaurant. Stylish dishes and hard-to-find wines. Prices are lower at the also fine Marché Café. *296 East Fifth Avenue; 541-342-3612. French.* **$$$**

MCMINNVILLE
Nick's Italian Cafe. Fixed-price five-course dinners; many local wines on the list. *521 NE Third Street; 503-434-4471. Italian.* **$$$**

SALEM
Alessandro's 120. May have the best wine list in town. *120 Commercial Street NE; 503-391-1774. Italian.* **$$**

Kwan's Cuisine. First in the area to serve local salmon in a black-bean sauce. *Mission and Commercial Streets; 503-362-7711. Eclectic.* **$$**

McGrath's Fish House. Statewide chain with good wine list; burgers, pastas, steaks, seafood. *350 Chemeketa Street NE; 503-362-0736. American.* **$–$$**

YAMHILL
Yamhill Cafe. Comfort food. *240 South Maple Street; 503-662-3504. American.* **$$**

■ UMPQUA VALLEY

ROSEBURG
Dino's Ristorante Italiano & Wine Bar. The restaurant doubles as a winery tasting room. *404 SE Jackson Street; 541-673-5383. Italian.* **$$**

Nick's Italian Cafe in McMinnville is a longtime Wine Country favorite.

La Garza Cellars. Dine on tasty, reasonably priced dishes, right at the winery. *491 Winery Lane; 541-679-9654. Contemporary.* **$**

White Rhino Restaurant. Lunch amid the animals at Wildlife Safari. *Safari Road off Lookingglass Road (I-5 Exit 119); 541-679-6761. American.* **$–$$**

■ ROGUE RIVER VALLEY

Ashland Creek Bar & Grill. Burgers and other comfort food. *92 North Main Street; 541-482-4131. American.* **$**

Chateaulin. A cozy bistro, one of the town's best restaurants. *50 East Main Street; 541-482-2264. French.* **$$–$$$**

Il Giardino. Pastas, steaks, seafood. *5 Granite Street; 541-488-0816. Italian.* **$–$$**

Macaroni's Ristorante. Pizzas, pastas, calzones, et cetera. *58 East Main Street; 541-488-3359. Italian.* **$**

Monet Restaurant and Garden. Country and traditional dishes, as conceived by a Rhône Valley chef. *36 South Second Street; 541-482-1339. French.* **$$–$$$**

Hamilton River House. Riverside setting for fresh fish and seafood, steaks, and other dishes. *1936 Rogue River Highway; 541-479-3938. American.* **$$**

River Rock Cafe. Soups, sandwiches. *966 SW Sixth Street; 541-479-7204. American.* **$**

Wild River Brewing & Pizza Co. Pub grub. *595 NE E Street; 541-471-7487. American.* **$**

Jacksonville Inn. Excellent food, superb wine list. Lighter dishes are served in the Bistro Lounge. *175 East California Street; 541-899-1900. Continental.* **$$$**

New Sammy's Cowboy Bistro. Simple but elegant country cookery. *2210 Pacific Highway; 541-535-2779. Contemporary.* **$$–$$$**

■ LODGING

Because the Oregon Wine Country is a relatively new destination, it does not yet have luxury lodgings to rival those of California's wine regions. There are some B&Bs (mostly in the northern Willamette Valley) and a few well-appointed lodges (in the Umpqua-Rogue region), but most wine country visitors stay in the region's major cities, all of which are close to vineyards. Below are some reservation services that can help you find a place, followed by a few of this author's recommendations and a list of chains that operate in western Oregon.

PRICE DESIGNATIONS FOR LODGING, PER COUPLE
$= less than $100   **$$** = $100–$150   **$$$** = 150–$200   **$$$$** = over $200

■ RESERVATION SERVICES

Karen Brown's Guides. *www.karenbrown.com/pnw.*

Oregon Bed & Breakfast Guild. *800-944-6196. www.obbg.org.*

A Pacific Reservation Service. *206-439-7677 or 800-684-2932; www.seattlebedandbreakfast.com.*

Unique Northwest Inns. *877-286-4783; www.uniqueinns.com.*

■ INNS AND SMALL HOTELS

PORTLAND

Heathman Hotel. A beautifully appointed hotel with a prime downtown location near museums, theaters, and restaurants. *1001 SW Broadway. 503-241-4100 or 800-551-0011. 150 rooms.* **$$$**

Portland's White House. Four-poster beds are among the comforts at this stately old Greek Revival home in northeastern Portland. Breakfasts here are big and delectable. *1914 NE Second Avenue; 503-287-7131. 9 rooms* **$–$$$**

RiverPlace Hotel. Some of the rooms at this pleasant, modern hotel overlook the Willamette River and its boating activities. *1510 SW Harbor Way; 503-228-3233 or 800-227-1333. 83 rooms.* **$$$–$$$$**

The tasting room of Del Rio Vineyards occupies a former stagecoach hotel.

WILLAMETTE VALLEY

Greenwood Inn. In an area dominated by motels, the Greenwood, just minutes from wineries, stands out for its well-appointed rooms and reasonable prices. *10700 SW Allen Boulevard, Beaverton; 503-643-7444. 217 rooms.* **$**

Harrison House Bed & Breakfast. This tree-shaded home built in the late 1930s is set in a lovely garden only a few blocks from the Oregon State University campus. The furnishings are in the Colonial style. *295 SW Harrison Street, Corvallis; 541-752-6248 or 800-233-6248. 4 rooms.* **$$**

Wine Country Farm. Sip and sleep at the winery's B&B. You can also go horseback riding among the vineyards. *6855 NE Breyman Orchards Road, Dayton; 503-864-3446 or 800-261-3446. 9 rooms.* **$$**

Hotel Oregon. This historic brick edifice in downtown McMinnville is part of the McMenamins pub chain. Rooms come with private or shared baths. *310 NE Evans Street, McMinnville; 503-472-8427 or 888-472-8427. 42 rooms.* **$–$$**

Steiger Haus Bed & Breakfast. A modern cedar-shingled house, the inn is near Linfield College, where the International Pinot Noir Celebration takes place. *360 Wilson Street, McMinnville; 503-472-0821. 4 rooms.* **$–$$**

Youngberg Hill Inn. Vineyards surround this modern (1989) hilltop inn, built to take advantage of the view. Reserve well ahead of your visit. *10660 SW Youngberg Hill Road, McMinnville; 503-472-2727 or 888-657-8668. 7 rooms.* **$$$–$$$$**

Marquee House. In a quiet woodsy corner on the banks of Mill Creek, this 1930s Colonial-style lodging is within walking distance of the state capitol, Willamette University, and Salem's historic district. *333 Wyatt Court Northeast, Salem. 503-391-0837 or 800-949-0837. 5 rooms.* **$**

UMPQUA

Hokanson's Guest House. A bit uphill from downtown, this 1882 Gothic Revival house is listed on the National Register of Historic Places. *848 SE Jackson Street, Roseburg; 541-672-2632 or 877-664-7760. 2 rooms.* **$**

Steamboat Inn. This very popular inn perches high above the North Umpqua River, in the Umpqua National Forest. *42705 North Highway 138, Steamboat; 541-498-2230 or 800-840-8825. 19 cabins, cottages, suites, and houses.* **$$$–$$$$**

ROGUE RIVER VALLEY

Ashland Springs Hotel. Built in 1925, the town's most elegant hotel, now operated by the WestCoast chain, has a two-story lobby with a large fireplace. *212 East Main Street, Ashland; 541-488-1700. 70 rooms.* **$$$**

Chateau at the Oregon Caves. This rustic lodge, built in 1935 of local materials, with Arts and Crafts furniture throughout, spans a ravine at Oregon Caves National Monument. It's close to Illinois Valley wineries. *20000 Caves Highway, Cave Junction; 541-592-3400. 22 rooms.* **$**

Under the Greenwood Tree. This restored 1862 house is set amid beautiful gardens—with a garden chandelier and outdoor wooden dance floor, among other pleasures—and surrounded by a 10-acre farm. *3045 Bellinger Lane, Medford; 541-776-0000 or 800-766-8099. 5 rooms.* **$$–$$$**

Morrison's Rogue River Lodge. A fishing guide built this lodge outside Grants Pass in 1946. It's a grand spot to come and fish by day and dine and sleep elegantly by night. *8500 Galice Road, Merlin; 541-476-3825. 13 cottages and rooms.* **$$**

■ HOTEL AND MOTEL CHAINS

Best Western. *800-528-1234; www.bestwestern.com.*
Comfort Inn. *800-228-5150; www.comfortinn.com.*
Days Inn. *800-325-2525; www.daysinn.com.*
Doubletree. *800-222-8733; www.doubletree.com.*
Embassy Suites. *800-362-2779; www.embassysuites.com.*
Hilton. *800-445-8667; www.hilton.com.*
Holiday Inn. *800-465-4329; www.6c.com.*
La Quinta. *800-531-5900; www.lq.com.*
Marriott. *800-228-9290; www.marriott.com.*
Quality Inns. *800-228-5151; www.qualityinn.com.*
Radisson. *800-333-3333; www.radisson.com.*
Ramada Inns. *800-272-6232; www.ramada.com.*
Sheraton. *800-325-3535; www.sheraton.com.*
Shilo Inns. *800-222-2244; www.shiloinns.com.*
Travelodge. *800-255-3050; www.travelodge.com.*
WestCoast. *800-325-4000; www.westcoasthotels.com.*

■ OFFICIAL TOURISM INFORMATION

Oregon. *800-547-7842; www.traveloregon.com.*
Eugene. *541-682-5010; www.ci.eugene.or.us.*
Medford. *541-779-4847 or 800-469-6307; www.visitmedford.org.*
Portland. *877-678-5263; www.travelportland.com.*
Portland. *800-962-3700. www.pova.com.*
Roseburg. *541-672-9731 or 800-444-9584; www.visitroseburg.com.*
Salem. *503-588-6161; www.cityofsalem.net.*
Southern Oregon Visitors Association. *541-779-4691; www.sova.org.*

■ WINE ASSOCIATIONS

Oregon Wine. *541-752-7418; www.oregon-wine.com.*
Oregon Wine Advisory Board. *503-228-8336; www.oregonwine.org.*
Oregon Winegrower's Association. *503-228-8403; www.oregonwinegrowers.org.*
Southern Oregon Winery Association. *800-781-9463; www.sorwa.org.*
Yamhill County Wineries Association. *503-646-2985; www.yamhillwine.com.*

■ RESOURCES/WEB SITES

Douglas County Museum of History and Natural History. Outstanding collection of local artifacts and history; incipient historical research on local vineyards and wineries. *541-957-7007; www.co.douglas.or.us/museum.*

Oregon Historical Society. Excellent museum of Oregon history and artifacts, with a very fine bookstore. *503-222-1741; www.ohs.org.*

OregonLive.com. News and features from the statewide *Oregonian* newspaper, plus Web-only listings and resources. *www.oregonlive.com.*

Oregon Wine and Farm Tour. A guide to southern Oregon farms and wineries. *541-512-2955; www.oregonwineandfarmtour.com.*

Southern Oregon Historical Society. Local artifacts, including wine-related ones. *541-773-6536; www.sohs.org.*

***Willamette Week* Online.** Portland-based alternative weekly provides news, dining, nightlife, arts and other coverage. *www.wweek.com.*

■ Shipping Wine

Sending wine home from the wineries you visit is getting easier as more states are liberalizing the rules for shipping wine interstate as a result of legislative actions and court decisions. In 2003, Virginia, North Carolina, and South Carolina opened their borders to direct-to-consumer shipments of wine from other states. Texas also allowed shipments, though only to "wet" counties. Currently, many states, including California, Oregon, and Washington, allow residents to accept at least some out-of-state wine deliveries.

Laws regarding the purchase of wines online have also begun to liberalize. In 2003, many states began allowing shipments, and, depending on the outcome of several court cases, including ones in Florida, Michigan, and New York, online wine shipping could expand.

Because laws about interstate shipping of wine vary so greatly from state to state—and because the penalties for noncompliance in some states can be severe—if you're going to ship wine home, it is wise to do so either through the winery or a professional shipper.

The Elizabethan Stage is the largest of the three theaters in which the Oregon Shakespeare Festival's productions take place.

■ Festivals and Events

■ February

Newport Seafood and Wine Festival. The granddaddy of Oregon's wine and seafood fests, with fresh seafood, food and wine pairings, commercial and amateur wine competitions, and arts and crafts. *541-265-8801.*

Oregon Shakespeare Festival, Ashland. The renowned drama festival runs from late February until early November. *541-482-4331; www.osfashland.org.*

The Oregon Wine and Food Festival, Salem. Wineries show off their wares; there are also cooking demonstrations and arts and crafts. *503-580-2509.*

■ March

McMinnville Wine & Food Classic. This fundraising event for St. James Catholic School is one of the Wine Country's most popular festivals, with participation by local wineries and guest chefs from well-known regional restaurants. There's music and entertainment too. *503-472-4033; www.macwfc.org.*

■ April

Astoria-Warrenton Crab and Seafood Festival, Astoria. A classic seafood fest, with fresh crab and other local seafoods, crab races, entertainment, a crafts show, and the output of 40-plus local wineries. *800-875-6807; www.oldoregon.com.*

Umpqua Valley Barrel Tasting Bus Tour. On this fun tour of seven Umpqua Valley wineries, there are new releases to sample and food to eat at every stop. *541-672-9731 or 800-444-9584; www.visitroseburg.com.*

■ May

Annual Greatest of the Grape, Canyonville. Umpqua Valley event that includes wine-tasting, a dinner, entertainment, and a fine-arts auction. *541-673-7575.*

Arts in Bloom Festival, Medford. This open-air event celebrates spring with art, flowers, local food and wine, entertainers. *541-608-8524; www.visitmedford.org.*

Yamhill County Memorial Day Weekend in the Wine Country. Many wineries not ordinarily open to the public hold open houses. Come early—popular wineries can get crowded. *503-646-2985; www.yamhillwine.com.*

■ **June**

Britt Festivals, Jacksonville. Running from June until September, the Britt Festivals include performances by internationally known classical, jazz, and pop musicians in an outdoor theater. *541-779-0847; www.brittfest.org.*

Wineries of Lane County Summer Barrel Tour. Take a one- or two-day bus tour to wineries and vineyards (some of them seldom open to the public) in the Eugene area. Appetizers are served with the wines. Reservations required. *800-992-8499.*

■ **July**

Art and the Vineyard, Eugene. Three-days of wine- and food-tasting make up this annual event in Alton Baker Park, but the spotlight is on the marketplace, where more than 100 artists set up shop. *541-485-2221; www.artandthevineyard.org.*

International Pinot Noir Celebration, McMinnville. A major event among those dedicated to a single grape, this attracts growers, winemakers, and consumers from all over the world—and it's hard to get into. Separate tickets for the concluding Afternoon of Pinot Noir are easier to come by. *800-775-4762; www.ipnc.org.*

Land of Umpqua Wine Festival, Roseburg. Oregon's oldest continual wine festival has been moved from September to July (and to Roseburg's Stewart Park). Local wines, entertainment, food, and arts and crafts are on the bill. Reservations are necessary for the Friday-night dinner. *541-672-2648; www.visitroseburg.com.*

■ **August**

Rogue Valley Balloon Rally, Medford. Hot-air balloon extravaganza at the Rogue Valley International Airport includes mass ascensions and night-glow ballooning, as well as food and wine. *541-608-8524; www.visitmedford.org.*

■ **November**

¡Salud!, Dundee and Portland. Oregon's Pinot Noir Auction raises money to provide health care and other services for the state's seasonal vineyard workers. *503-681-1850; www.saludauction.org.*

Yamhill County Thanksgiving Weekend in the Wine Country. The second of two annual events when many wineries not ordinarily open to the public hold open houses with food and entertainment. *503-646-2985; www.yamhillwine.com.*

G L O S S A R Y

Acidity. The tartness of a wine, derived from the fruit acids of the grape. Acids stabilize a wine (i.e., keep it from going flat), serving as a counterpoint to its sugars, if there are any, and bringing out its flavors. Acid is to wine what salt is to cooking—a proper amount is necessary, but too much spoils the taste. Tartaric acid is the major acid in wine, but malic, lactic, and citric acids also occur, in greatly variable concentrations.

Aftertaste. The way a wine lingers on the palate after you have swirled it around in your mouth. Good wines have a long-lasting aftertaste, with many complex flavors and aromas.

Aging. The process by which wines react to oxygen at a very slow rate. Wine is most commonly aged in oak vats or in old or new oak barrels, slowly interacting with the air through the pores in the wood. If properly stored, some wines improve with aging, becoming smoother and more complex and developing a pleasing bouquet. New oak contains tannins and flavoring elements that the wine leaches from the wood. Too much exposure to these oak extracts can overpower the varietal character of a wine. Most wines do not age well. Even a small amount of oxidation can spoil lighter wines, which are much more enjoyable when young and fresh. When aged for just a short time, they may lose their fruit and thus their appeal. Their color dulls: whites turn brownish, rosés orange, reds brown. Today even some of the wines once made in a heavier style—e.g., cabernet sauvignon—are sometimes made to be drunk after 5 to 10 rather than 20 to 50 years.

Alcohol. Ethyl alcohol is a colorless, volatile, pungent spirit that gives wine its stimulating effect and some of its flavor, and acts as a preservative, stabilizing the wine and allowing it to age. Alcohol content must be stated on the label, expressed as a percentage of volume, except when a wine is designated table wine (*see* Table Wine).

American Viticultural Area (AVA). An AVA is a region with unique soil, climate, and other grape-growing conditions designated as such by the Alcohol Tobacco Tax and Trade Bureau. The term is basically synonymous with "appellation," though

appellation sometimes refers colloquially to a wine region that has no legal geographical standing. When a label lists an appellation—e.g., Rogue River Valley—85 percent of the grapes the wine is made from must come from that region.

Appellation. *See* American Viticultural Area.

Applegate Valley. An AVA within southern Oregon's larger Rogue River Valley AVA, warmer and drier than the Illinois Valley to the west but cooler and moister than the Bear Creek Valley to the east. Grape varieties planted here include chardonnay, cabernet sauvignon, merlot, and zinfandel.

Argol. A crude form of tartar, often deposited on the sides of wine barrels during aging.

Arneis. An white-wine grape cultivated in the Piedmont region of Italy. In Oregon it has been planted by Ponzi Vineyards with excellent results.

Aroma. The scent of young wine derived directly from the fresh fruit. It diminishes with fermentation and is replaced by a more complex bouquet as the wine ages. The term may also be used to describe special fruity odors in a wine, like black cherry, green olive, ripe raspberry, or apple.

Assemblage. *See* Blending.

Astringent. A wine's sour taste. Experts, however, use the term "sour" only for a spoiled wine.

AVA. *See* American Viticultural Area.

Baco Noir. A red French-American hybrid grape that can produce smoky-flavored wines with no hint of foxiness. Sparingly planted in western Oregon.

Balance. The harmony of elements in a wine. A well-balanced wine has a special mouth feel, a simultaneous appeal to the olfactory, gustatory, and tactile senses.

Barrel. A cylindrical storage container with bulging sides; usually made from American, French, Slavonic, or Baltic oak. A full barrel holds the equivalent of 240 regular 750 ml bottles.

Barrel Fermenting. The fermenting of wine in small oak barrels instead of large tanks or vats, allowing the winemaker to keep grape lots separate before blending them. This method, traditionally used by small European wineries, has recently become popular among West Coast winemakers; the trend may or may not survive the spiraling cost of oak barrels.

Bear Creek Valley. A winemaking district of the Rogue River Valley AVA, branching off from the Rogue River Valley just north of Central Point and stretching southeast past Ashland to the foothills of the Siskiyou Mountains. It includes the lower slopes of the Cascade Mountain foothills to the east and of the Siskiyou Mountains to the west. This valley gets quite hot in summer, and is well suited to the ripening of cabernet sauvignon, cabernet franc, merlot, malbec, sauvignon blanc, and syrah, but chardonnay and pinot gris also do well in some of its cooler vineyards.

Big. The quality of having considerable body, forward aromas, and high alcohol. Big wines are not necessarily good wines, however, because the excess can make the flavors coarse and heavy.

Binning. Cellaring bottles of wine at the winery for aging. The bottles should be laid on their sides to keep the corks moist, since dried-out corks may allow air to leak in, spoiling the wine. Storage temperature and humidity should be kept as even as possible.

Wildflowers blossom next to the vineyards at Sokol Blosser in Yamhill County.

Blending. The careful mixing of several wines to create a wine of greater complexity—or a more enjoyable one, as when a heavy wine is blended with a lighter one to create a more readily approachable medium-bodied wine. Not all wines containing more than one grape variety are blends. In the vineyards of Bordeaux and in some Oregon vineyards, different varieties of grapes are interplanted and crushed together; this mixing is not considered a blending, since it occurs before the wine is fermented. The blending of sparkling wines is called *assemblage.*

Blush Wine. Pink wine, usually sweet and with little character, made from prime red-wine grapes that cannot find a market as red wine. Many so-called white zinfandels are actually blush wines. Better pink wines are usually labeled rosés.

Body. The substance of a wine as experienced by the palate. A full body is an advantage in the case of some reds, a disadvantage in many lighter whites.

Bordeaux Blend. A blend of red-grape varieties native to France's Bordeaux region—cabernet sauvignon, cabernet franc, malbec, merlot, and petit verdot—designed to make wines more well-rounded and complex.

Bottle Sizes. Metric sizes have replaced the traditional bottle sizes of gallon, quart, fifth, et al., though the old names linger:

Tenth . . . . .375 ml. of wine

Fifth . . . . .750 ml. (25.4 oz.)
The most commonly used wine bottle

Magnum . . . .1.50 liters (50.72 oz.)

Half Gallon . . .1.75 liters (59.2 oz.)

Double Magnum . . . . .3.0 liters
also called Jeroboam

Rehoboam . . . . .4.5 liters (approx.)
The equivalent of five 750 ml. bottles

Other, larger-sized bottles include the approximately 9-liter Salmanzar and the Nebuchadnezzar, which holds from 13 to 15 liters of wine, depending on where, when, and by whom it was made.

Bouquet. The odors a mature wine gives off when opened. The bouquet should be diverse but pleasing, complex but not confused, and should give an indication of the wine's grape variety, origin, age, and quality.

Brix. A method of telling whether grapes are ready for picking by measuring their sugars. Multiplying the

Brix number by .55 yields the potential alcohol content of the wine (though the finished wine may be slightly higher or lower).

Brut. A dry sparkling wine. *See also* Demi-sec, Sec.

Butt. A large wine barrel or cask with a capacity of 100 to 140 gallons; the most common holds 500 liters (132 U.S. gallons).

Cabernet Franc. A noble grape of France's Bordeaux region that produces aromatic red wines that are softer and subtler than those of the closely related cabernet sauvignon and that age more quickly. Cabernet franc is often blended into cabernet sauvignon to soften the wine of that somewhat harsher grape. In southern Oregon, where it has been planted only recently, cabernet franc yields excellent, well-balanced wine.

Cabernet Sauvignon. The noble red-wine grape that has made the clarets of Bordeaux renowned, it grows very well in the warmer vineyards of southern Oregon's Umpqua and Rogue River Valleys. Its wine is deeply red and tannic and can require a long period of aging to become enjoyable. For this reason it is often blended with cabernet franc, merlot, and other related red varieties, to

soften the resulting wine and to make it enjoyable earlier.

Case. A carton of twelve 750 ml. bottles of wine. A magnum case contains six 1.5-liter magnum bottles.

Cask. A wine container, commonly made from oak staves.

Champagne. *See* Sparkling Wines.

Chardonnay. The noble French grape variety of the great white Burgundies from Montrachet, Meursault, and Chablis, as well as the lesser whites of Pouilly-Fuissé and Mâcon. It is also one of the principal varieties of the Champagne region. It is widely planted in Oregon, where it tends to make a pleasant seafood or sipping wine but not a great one—a limitation the state's winemakers are trying to overcome by planting promising new clones.

Chehalem Ridge/Chehalem Valley. A hilly region west of Newberg and north of the Dundee Hills. The lowlands bordering the Chehalem Mountains are becoming known as both the Chehalem Valley and the Willakenzie District, the latter because of the Willakenzie-type soils that dominate the area. The pinot noir grapes grown on these soils have deep earth flavors with a touch of blackberry and tree fruits. Acclaimed

producers include Beaux Frères, Chehalem, Brick House, and Patricia Green Cellars.

Chenin Blanc. A noble old French white-grape variety that has recently fallen from grace because it does not make big wine, as chardonnay does. But in Oregon it makes excellent fruity white wine that in good years may be aged and can develop a beautiful, complex bouquet.

Chilling. A common practice for sparkling wines and some whites, decried for reds by traditionalists, but indulged in by some very famous winemakers on hot summer days. (So if you'd like an ice cube in your wine—put it in!)

Claret. A name once applied to red wines from Bordeaux that were shipped to Britain's discriminating wine connoisseurs. The term came into disrepute after it was applied to bulk wines. It is, however, regaining respect as premium wineries bestow the name on their red blends.

Clarity. The lack of particles—both large and minute—floating in a wine; a requirement for a good wine. Wine should always be clear (though it can be dark or dense); it should never be cloudy.

Cloudiness. The presence of particles—often minute—that do not settle out of a wine, causing it to taste dusty or even muddy. To correct it, set the bottle, at a slant, in a place where it will not be disturbed, then let the sediments settle. This could take from a few minutes to several hours depending on the wine. Decant the clear liquid on top and discard the sediments. If the wine remains cloudy, get rid of it—it has been badly made or is spoiled.

Complexity. Layers of different flavors and aromas in harmony with the overall balance of a wine, and perhaps, in an aged wine, a pleasing bouquet and a lingering aftertaste.

Controlled Fermentation. Fermentation at low temperatures, in chilled tanks, to preserve the fruit and delicacy of the grape flavors and aromas in white wines. Reds may undergo uncontrolled fermentation, which results in high temperatures that help extract tannins and pigments from the grape skins, but this is undesirable for whites.

Cooperage. A collective term used to describe all the containers of a winery in which wine is stored and aged before bottling. It includes barrels, casks, vats, and tanks of different materials and sizes.

Corky. Used to describe a wine affected by off flavors and aromas created by a leaky cork or cork infection. The contact between the wine and the air that such leakage allows will, with time, spoil the wine.

Crush. Colloquial West Coast winemaker's term denoting the vintage in which grapes are made into wine. Not all grapes grown go into wine. Some go to market fresh, others are made into raisins; these are not part of the crush but are counted as part of the grape harvest.

Cuvée. A sparkling wine that is a blend of different wines and sometimes different vintages. Most sparkling wines are cuvées, although in very good years some are vintage dated.

Decant. To slowly and carefully pour an aged wine from its bottle into a decanter. Decanting needs be done only with old wines that have a sediment, which, when stirred up by careless handling, might cloud the wine. When wine has been carefully decanted, the sediment remains in the bottle.

Demi-sec. Although *sec* means "dry," in the convoluted language of sparkling wine, *demi-sec* is sweet. More specifically, wine that contains 3.5 to 5 percent sugar.

Dessert Wines. Sweet wines that are big in flavor and aroma but may be quite low in alcohol, or wines that have been fortified (*see* fortification) with brandy or neutral spirits and may be quite high (17–21 percent) in alcohol.

Dolcetto. A red-wine grape from the Piedmont region of Italy, now grown in the Umpqua Valley, where it makes lush, supple, easily enjoyable wines.

Dosage. A mixture of wine and sugar added to fermented wine in order to create bubbles, inducing a secondary fermentation in the bottle. *See* Sparkling Wines.

Dundee, Red Hills of. *See* Red Hills of Dundee.

Dry. The term used to describe a wine that is not sweet, although it may contain some residual sugar. The American wine industry's long fight to wean consumers away from sweet wines has turned "dry" into an important enological concept.

Eola Hills. A range of low rolling hills in the mid–Willamette Valley, northwest of Salem and west of the Willamette River. Their south-facing slopes harbor many of Oregon's best vineyards. Top producers include

Bethel Heights, Cristom, Evesham Wood, Firesteed, Witness Tree, and, in the northern section known as the Amity Hills, Amity and Tempest. Pinot noir grapes grown here—and eagerly sought out by winemakers from other regions—are characterized by rich blackberry and black currant flavors.

Estate Bottled. A label term indicating that the winery and the vineyards from which the grapes were harvested are in the same appellation (which must be printed on the label); that the winery owns or controls the vineyards; and that all the wine-making processes, from crushing to bottling, were done at a single winery facility.

Fermentation. The process—in which enzymes generated by yeast cells convert the grape sugars of must into alcohol and carbon dioxide—by which grape juice becomes wine. (*See also* Controlled Fermentation.)

Fermenter. Any vessel, small or large (such as a barrel, tank, or vat), in which wine is fermented.

Filtering, Filtration. A purification process in which wine is pumped through filters to rid it of suspended particles. If mishandled, filtration can remove a wine's flavor.

Fining. A traditional method of clarifying wine by adding crushed eggshells, isinglass, or other natural substances to a barrel. As these solids settle to the bottom, they take suspended particles with them, thus clarifying the wine. A slower, more tedious process than filtering, but one that makes better wine.

Flat. Said of a wine that lacks acid and is thus dull; also of a sparkling wine that has lost its bubbles.

Fortification. A process by which brandy or natural spirits are added to a wine to stop fermentation and to increase its level of alcohol, making it more stable—less subject to spoilage and to separation of the solids from the liquids—than a regular table wine after a bottle has been opened. Before the modern American wine revolution, most Northwest wines were fortified.

Foxiness. The odd flavor of native American grapes or their hybrids, including Catawba, Concord, and Island Belle (Campbell Early). Wines made from these grapes are an acquired taste.

Free Run. Juice that runs from the crushed grapes before pressing. It is more intense in flavor than pressed juice and has fewer (or no) off flavors.

Fruity. Having aromatic nuances of fresh fruit—fig, raspberry, apple, et cetera. Fruitiness, a sign of quality in young wines, is replaced by bouquet in aged wines.

Fumé Blanc. Term coined by the Napa Valley's Robert Mondavi to describe a dry, crisp oak-aged sauvignon blanc. It is now used so indiscriminately by wineries in both California and Oregon that it has lost any special meaning, though a wine so labeled will almost certainly contain sauvignon blanc. It may be blended with sémillon or not.

Gamay. Also called Gamay Beaujolais, this vigorous French red-grape variety produces pleasant reds and rosés that should be drunk young. It is sparingly planted in Oregon, and there is some confusion as to which West Coast plantings are the true gamay and which are in fact clones of pinot noir.

Gewürztraminer. A German-Alsatian pinkish grape variety that makes excellent aromatic, almost spicy white wine in Oregon.

Gravity-flow winery. A winery at which grapes are crushed at the top level and their juice allowed to flow down to the fermenters and, later, to the storage barrels or vats by the natural force of gravity alone. The method has gained popularity among winemakers who feel that pumps can damage the freshly released must and/or allow excessive oxygen to enter it, increasing the danger of spoilage.

Green. Said of a wine made from unripe grapes, with a pronounced leafy flavor and a raw edge.

Grenache. A southern French red-wine grape of Spanish origin (*garnacha*), with limited plantings in western Oregon, where it makes good reds. Its popularity had declined in recent years but is once again increasing as wines made from this grape are being vinified in bigger, more complex style than that of the light reds of the recent past.

Horizontal Tasting. A tasting of wines of the same vintage from several wineries.

Huxelrebe. A German hybrid grape variety that ripens well in cool climates. Though it makes rather bland wine in hot climates, it can also make very good sweet, late-harvest wines. It is vinified by Chateau Lorane in the Southern Willamette Valley.

Illinois Valley. The westernmost section of the Rogue River Valley AVA. Marine air makes it cooler than the

Applegate and Bear Creek Valleys to the east. It is planted largely to chardonnay, muscat, gewürztraminer, pinot blanc, pinot gris, and pinot noir. Foris is the best local producer.

Johannisberg Riesling. *See* Riesling.

Late Harvest, Select Late Harvest, Special Select Late Harvest. Wine made from grapes harvested later in the fall than the main lot, and thus higher in sugar levels. These terms are vague, however, and have no legal meaning in Oregon; at worst, they may simply indicate that the grapes grew too ripe and that the resulting wine is sweet and cloying. Elk Cove and Sokol Blosser have made excellent late-harvest Rieslings from Yamhill County grapes.

Laterite. A porous soil, with a high aluminum and ferrous hydroxide content, covering much of northwestern Oregon; it is a prized vineyard soil in the Red Hills of Dundee.

Lees. The spent yeast and any grape solids that have dropped out of suspension while a wine ages in a barrel or tank. White left on the lees for a time improves in complexity; this method has become a popular way of aging chardonnay and sauvignon blanc.

Leon Millot. Red French-American hybrid grape, more vigorous than Maréchal Foch; it ripens even earlier and bears a heavier crop. The grape produces a Burgundy-like still wine that can be very dark and very good. Sparingly planted in western Oregon.

Maderized. A term applied to a white or rosé wine that is past its prime and has become oxidized with an undesirable flavor and aroma of Madeira, the Portuguese fortified wine.

Malbec. A red Bordeaux grape commonly used in blending. In southern Oregon it makes well-structured wines, as in the superb malbec produced by the Umpqua Valley's Abacela Winery.

Malolactic Fermentation. A secondary fermentation in the tank or barrel that changes harsh malic acid into softer lactic acid and carbon dioxide, making the wine smoother. Because it lowers the perceptible level of a wine's acids, malolactic fermentation is frowned upon in regions where wines, especially whites, tend to have low acid to begin with. In cool regions, where wines have a high natural acidity, it is a boon to the winemaker, because it rounds out the wine, making it less acidic and more complex at the same time.

Maréchal Foch. Early-ripening red French-American hybrid. Produces large amounts of gamay-like clusters that produce Burgundy-style wine, but with less finesse and elegance. Can be made into intensely concentrated (though somewhat vulgar) wine in the Australian shiraz style. Planted in western Oregon.

Mélon. A French white-wine grape from the western end of the Loire valley (Muscadet), where it makes a dry, tart wine. Wines made from Oregon plantings are generally more full-bodied and complex. Panther Creek Winery produces an excellent one. The grape is more correctly known as mélon de bourgogne, though it has not been planted in its Burgundian homeland for a long time.

Merlot. Known in its native France as *merlot noir*, for the dark, blue-black color of its berries, this grape is more productive than cabernet and gives a softer, more supple wine that may be drunk at a younger age. It grows well in southern Oregon.

Méthode Champenoise. *See* Sparkling Wines.

Meunier. Also called Pinot Meunier, this dusty black grape is made mostly into white or off-white sparkling wine. A relative of pinot noir, it is more productive than that grape but not as high in quality. While there are limited plantings in the Pacific Northwest, it may have been one of the earliest grapes planted in Oregon's Willamette Valley, cultivated by French-Canadian trappers who had retired from service with the Hudson's Bay Company and settled near Champoeg.

Müller-Thurgau. A German vinifera hybrid widely planted in western Oregon and other Pacific Northwest vineyards. Popular in Oregon, it makes a pleasant white wine with a muscatel flavor, which can resemble Rieslings grown in coastal climes.

Muscat Ottonel. An Alsatian grape variety planted in western Oregon, where it makes light, somewhat spicy wine.

Must. Crushed grapes or their juice, either ready to be or in the process of being fermented into wine.

Nebbiolo. The great red-wine grape of Italy's Piedmont region, where it makes such renowned wines as barolo, barbaresco, and gattinara. Its sturdy, full-bodied wine is fairly high in alcohol and ages splendidly. It is famous for the hints of tar and tobacco in its undertaste (a positive attribute in red wine) and for its peppery spiciness.

Nebbiolo, like other Italian reds but unlike French-style reds, does better in old than in new oak. In recent years it has been successfully planted in western Oregon.

Noble. A term that, applied to grapes and wines, denotes both inherited status and quality. A noble grape variety produces good (or, in the right hands, great) wine almost everywhere it is planted. A noble wine—either varietal or blended—is one whose combination of flavors, aromas, mouth feel, and finish even a novice can identify as special.

Noble Rot. *Botrytis cinerea,* a beneficial fungus mold that attacks certain ripe grapes, perforating their skin. This shrivels the grapes through dehydration and concentrates the sugars and flavor elements in the remaining juice while preserving the grape's acids. This helps keep the resulting sweet wine from becoming cloying.

Non-Vintage. Having no vintage date on the label—usually indicating that the wine is a blend from different vineyards, growing regions, and even vintages. This is not necessarily evidence of poor quality; it may represent an attempt to make wine of a consistent, recognizable quality year after year.

Nose. The overall fragrance (aroma or bouquet) given off by a wine, which is the better part of its flavor.

Oak. The most popular wood for making wine barrels, because, if used properly, it can impart desirable flavors to the wine stored in it and add to its complexity. If abused, it can make a wine taste oaky or woody.

Oaky. Said of a wine that has been aged in new oak for too long and tastes more of the vanilla-like flavors of the wood than of the grape. Once praised as a virtue in California chardonnays; now considered a fault.

Oregon Oak. Oregon white oak, *Quercus garryana,* used increasingly to make wine barrels.

Oxidized. Condition of a wine that had too much contact with the air, either as juice or through faulty winemaking or a leaky barrel or cork. Most often occurs with white wine, although it does happen to reds too. An oxidized wine has lost its freshness and is on its way to becoming maderized. Depending on how far the oxidation has progressed, such a wine should be either drunk immediately (preferably with strongly seasoned food) or discarded.

Pétillant. A French term indicating, like the German *spritzig,* a wine that is slightly sparkling. This quality can be refreshing in light silvaner, chenin blanc, or other chilled white carafe wine, as well as in Oregon muscats.

Petite Sirah. A noble red-wine grape of California whose origin is shrouded in mystery. It was once thought to be the true *syrah* grape of France, but it is not. Because it is a true vinifera grape, it may be a hybrid that occurred in a mid-19-century California vineyard—much like the equally mysterious zinfandel. It has recently been planted in eastern Washington and in Oregon, where it makes excellent red wine.

Petit Verdot. A red Bordeaux grape that is used mostly for blending but can yield full-bodied, deeply colored wines of great complexity. It needs heat to ripen properly, and is thus planted in some of southern Oregon's warmest vineyards.

pH. An indicator of a wine's acidity. It is a reverse measure—that is, the lower the pH level, the higher the acidity.

Phylloxera. A disease caused by the root louse *Phylloxera vastatrix,* native to the central and eastern United States. It attacks grapevine roots, first weakening, and ultimately destroying them. It was transported to France when the French experimented with native American grape varieties such as Concord and muscadine.

Pinot Blanc. A white-wine grape variety that evolved from pinot gris, which in turn evolved from pinot noir. Pinot blanc, when treated properly, makes a wine much like chardonnay. It is widely planted in western Oregon, where it makes pleasant white wine that goes well with seafood dishes.

Pinot Gris. The classic white grape of Alsace, Italy (where it's called pinot grigio) and Germany (Ruländer); a white mutation of pinot noir. Widely planted in western Oregon, where it makes an interesting and complex dry white wine. More recent vinifications have also included wines made in the lighter, fruitier pinot grigio style.

Pinot Noir. An ancient noble French grape variety that, under perfect conditions—often hard to achieve—makes some of the best red wine in the world. Oregon's signature grape, it is widely planted in the Willamette, Umpqua, and Rogue River Valleys, where in good years it produces world-class wines.

An allée of trees in the Red Hills of Dundee.

Pinot Noir Blanc. White wine made from the black pinot noir grape, most commonly as sparkling wine called *blanc de noirs.* "White" is relative here, since the wine, more often than not, has a rosy pink tinge.

Pomace. The spent skins and grape solids from which the juice has been pressed, commonly returned to the fields as fertilizer.

Racking. Moving wine from one tank or barrel to another, to leave deposits behind; the wine may or may not be fined or filtered in the process.

Red Hills of Dundee. The hills of north-central Yamhill County, famed for well-drained red laterite soils, which grow superior pinot gris and pinot noir. Many of Oregon's best-known wineries are here or in nearby Dundee, Carlton, or McMinnville: Archery Summit, Chateau Benoit, Domaine Drouhin, Domaine Serene, Ken Wright, Panther Creek, Rex Hill, Sokol Blosser. Red Hill–grown grapes tend to be brighter, leaning toward cherry and strawberry flavors, with a pleasant spiciness and a touch of earthy *terroir.*

Residual Sugar. Sugar left over from fermentation that is above the 0.5 percent threshold of perception. In the 1990s leaving it in became a popular way of finishing white and red table wines, because consumers, while claiming to like dry wines, actually prefer slightly sweet ones.

Riesling. Also called Johannisberg Riesling or white Riesling, the noble white-wine grape of Germany. This cool-climate grape can yield great wine in the Pacific Northwest, though it mostly produces indifferent sweet ones. It was introduced to the Wine Country of California in the middle of the 19th century by immigrant vintners and is now also planted in Oregon, eastern Washington, British Columbia, and, sparingly, in the Puget Sound region.

Rogue River Valley. A southern Oregon viticultural area that comprises the Bear Creek, Applegate, and Illinois Valley grape-growing regions just north of the California border. The valley can become very warm in summer, but the nights are cool, and the growing season is short due to the high elevation—mostly above 1,000 feet, higher than the other wine-growing areas in the state. The region's western section, only 15 miles from the Pacific Ocean, is cooled by marine air that flows up the river valleys and over low mountain passes.

Rosé. French term for pink wine, usually made from black (red-wine) grapes whose juice has been left on the skins only long enough to give it a tinge of color. Rosés can be pleasant and versatile food wines, especially when they are made from premium grapes like cabernet sauvignon, grenache, or pinot noir.

Rounded. Said of a well-balanced, complete wine—a good wine, though not necessarily a distinctive or great one.

Sangiovese. The main red grape of Italy's Chianti district and of much of central Italy. Depending on how it is grown and vinified, this versatile grape can be made into vibrant, light- to medium-bodied wines as well as into long-lived, very complex reds (like Italy's renowned Brunello di Montalcino). It has been planted successfully in western Oregon, where it makes medium-bodied, full-flavored wine.

Sauvignon Blanc. A white grape of France's Bordeaux region. It most likely thrived on the banks of the Gironde estuary long before the Romans introduced viticulture to southwestern France. Sauvignon blanc does well in southern Oregon,

where it makes very enjoyable wine. A dry, austere wine made from this grape—plain or blended with sémillon—is sometimes marketed as fumé blanc.

Sec. Although *sec* means "dry" in French, in speaking about wines sec indicates one that has from 1.7 to 3.5 percent sugar. In the language of sparkling wine, drier than demi-sec but not as dry as brut.

Sediment. Deposits that most red wines throw as they age in the bottle, thus clarifying their appearance, flavors, and aromas. Not a defect in an old wine or in a new wine that has been bottled unfiltered.

Sémillon. A white Bordeaux grape variety that, blended with sauvignon blanc, has made some of the best sweet wines in the world. Like the Riesling grape, it can be affected by the noble rot, which concentrates the juices and intensifies the flavors and aromas. It is planted in southern Oregon's Rogue River Valley, where it is often blended with sauvignon blanc to make fumé blanc–style wines.

Silvaner. Also known as sylvaner, this white-wine grape from Central Europe makes a good (if not great) greenish-yellow wine with a light body and aroma. Little of the grape is planted in the Pacific Northwest today. Like Riesling, silvaner has been largely replaced by more popular white-wine varieties such as chardonnay and sauvignon blanc. The short-lived Reuter's Hill winery made a delightful version in the early 1980s.

Southern Willamette Valley. The valley and foothill area west of Eugene, which has developed more slowly as a wine-growing area than have the central and northern Willamette Valleys, though its vineyards produce grapes of the highest quality. Secret House and Silvan Ridge have long made excellent but affordable wines here; King Estate Winery has planted extensive hillside vineyards southwest of Eugene. The pinot noir grapes grown here tend to have higher-toned flavors, marked in ripe years by a fine complexity and distinguished tannic structure, and lovely strawberry and cherry flavors. In warm years, the local chardonnays are loaded with tropical fruit flavors. Pinot gris also thrives in the warm, well-drained soils of the hills.

Sparkling Wines. Wines in which carbon dioxide is suspended, making them bubbly. Sparkling wines were invented in Champagne, France's northernmost wine district. Grapes in that area tend to be on the acidic side because they don't always ripen fully. For this reason, sparkling wines have traditionally been naturally tart, even austere. In America, the term Champagne is often used to denote sparkling wines of local origin, but the French frown on this, and indeed it is illegal to use the term in Oregon and British Columbia (though not in California or Washington). But the top sparkling wines of the Pacific Northwest are in no way inferior to their French counterparts.

Sparkling wines are traditionally made from pinot noir and chardonnay grapes (and in France from meunier as well). In Oregon, Riesling grapes may also be used. Sparkling wines with 1.5 percent sugar or less are labeled **brut**; those with 1.2–2 percent, **extra dry**; those with 1.7–3.5 percent, **sec**; those with 3.5–5 percent, **demi-sec**; and those with more than 5 percent, **doux**. A sparkling wine to which no dosage has been added will be bone dry and may be called **extra-brut** or **natural.**

Good sparkling wine will always be expensive, because a great deal of work goes into making it. Sparkling wines made in the traditional, time-consuming fashion may be labeled *méthode champenoise* or "fermented in this bottle." But read carefully. There is also sparkling wine labeled "wine made in the bottle," and there

is a great difference in methodology between *this* and *the*. The latter wine is made by the simpler, cheaper "transfer process," in which the sediments are filtered out. Filtered wines are less complex and their bubbles more sparingly distributed.

Stressing. A method of producing more intense wine by subjecting grapevines to adverse conditions. When forced to compete for sunlight, water, and nutrients, vines tend to produce smaller grapes that are more intense, with deeper flavor, than unstressed vines do. By contrast, grapes grown on rich, moist (or overly irrigated) bottomlands tend to be watery (i.e., overly juicy), with diluted or even off flavors. Grapevines have traditionally been planted on dry, well-drained hillsides or slopes; even in irrigated vineyards, quality growers make sure that their vines receive only the minimum moisture necessary. Grapevines can also be stressed by the removal of foliage or, some growers maintain, by planting vines very close together.

Sugar. Occurring naturally in grapes, sugar is the food the yeasts digest to make alcohol. The higher the sugar of the grape, the higher the potential alcohol of the wine. Fermentation stops when all the sugar has been

digested or when the alcohol level becomes high enough (from 15 to 16 percent) to kill off the yeasts. In France it is legal to add sugar to unfermented grape juice in order to raise the alcohol level of a wine; in Oregon it is not.

Syrah. A red-wine grape from France's hot-climate Rhône region, it produces the best wine when grown in austere soils; it loses its noble qualities when the vines are planted in fertile, irrigated bottomlands. At its best, the wine made from this grape is big-bodied and complex and needs to be aged to bring out its best qualities. Syrah is being widely planted in the Rogue River and Umpqua Valleys, where it yields great wines.

Table Wine. A wine that has at least 7 percent but not more than 14 percent alcohol by volume. Wines so labeled need not state their exact alcohol content. (The term is sometimes used, incorrectly, by consumers to denote an inexpensive wine.)

Tank. A very large container, usually upright and cylindrical, in which wine is fermented and stored. Tanks are commonly made of stainless steel, though they may also be made of wood or concrete (the latter are usually straight-sided cubicles) and lined with glass.

Tannins. Naturally occurring compounds in grape skins, seeds, and stems and in barrel oak that taste astringent and make the mouth pucker. Because tannins settle out in the natural sediments that red wine throws as it ages, older reds have fewer tannins than do younger ones.

Tartaric Acid, Tartrates. The principal acid of wine, some of which is deposited in the form of crystals (tartrates) as the wine settles in a cask. Sometimes, in unstable wines, tartrates are also deposited in the bottle, and since they look like tiny shards of glass (though they are not harmful), consumers may complain of "broken glass" in the wine.

Tempranillo. A Spanish red-wine grape that has been planted in Oregon's Umpqua Valley, where it makes deep-flavored, well-balanced wine. Abacela Winery, south of Roseburg, pioneered this grape and has made an outstanding Tempranillo Reserve from estate grapes.

Terroir. The French term for soil, used to indicate that the soil of a specific vineyard imparts a special taste to its grapes and, through them, to the finished wine. The term is also used—colloquially, and not altogether correctly—to indicate a specific microclimate.

Tocai Friulano. An Italian white-wine grape cultivated in the foothills of the Alps. It was recently planted by Adelsheim Vineyards in Yamhill County, where it makes a fine dry wine with a touch of elegance.

Umpqua Valley. An appellation that includes the middle courses of the Umpqua River and its tributaries around Roseburg. The valley is not a simple open basin like the Willamette Valley to the north; its many gently sloping hillsides and river drainages have led it to be known as the Hundred Valleys of the Umpqua. It is drier and warmer, and has a greater variety of soils, than the Willamette Valley. Many kinds of grapes thrive in the region's different microclimates, from chardonnay, pinot gris, pinot noir, and Riesling to cabernet sauvignon, dolcetto, malbec, merlot, and tempranillo. Top producers include Abacela, Henry Estate, HillCrest, and Melrose. Umpqua Valley red- and white-wine grapes are highly regarded, and regularly purchased by several Willamette Valley wineries.

Varietal Wine. A wine that takes its name not from a town, district, or vineyard—as in much of Europe—but from the grape variety from which it is made, such as chardonnay, merlot, or sangiovese. According to law, at least 75 percent of a wine labeled as a varietal must be made from the grape variety printed on the label.

Vat. A large container of stainless steel, wood, or concrete, often open at the top, in which wine is fermented or blended. The term is sometimes used interchangeably with "tank."

Vertical Tasting. A tasting of one or more varietal wines of different vintages, but from the same winery, generally starting with the youngest and proceeding to the oldest.

Vinifera. The great wine grapes of the Old World, which—despite their widely varying character—all belong to a single species, *Vitis vinifera*. Many varieties of vinifera grapes have been successfully transplanted to the New World, and they produce the best wines here. The native grapes of the New World tend to have odd flavors.

Vintage. The grape harvest, and the year in which the grapes are harvested. On the West Coast, the term "crush" may also be used for the harvest. A vintage date on a bottle always indicates the year in which the grapes were harvested—never the year in which the wine was bottled.

Viognier. A white-wine grape of France's Rhône Valley that produces a unique, distinguished golden wine with a fruity bouquet. It has recently been planted in western Oregon, where it promises to make excellent, complex wines.

Viticultural Area. *See* American Viticultural Area.

Walla Walla Valley. An appellation in eastern Oregon, shared with Washington. The Oregon portion has vineyards but no wineries.

White Pinot Noir. *See* Pinot Noir Blanc.

Willamette Valley. A large intermountain trough stretching for approximately 100 miles, from Eugene north to the Columbia River at Portland. Annual rainfall averages 40 inches, primarily during the winter months. Because it is protected by the Coast Range from the chill airs of the Pacific Coast, its summers are generally warm and dry and its autumns marked by warm days and cool nights—perfect weather for maturing grapes. The vast majority of Oregon vineyards are here; the majority of these are clustered at the northern end, in the Eola Hills and in Yamhill County.

Woody. A pejorative term, said of a wine that has been stored in a wooden barrel or cask for too long and has picked up excessive wood aromas and flavors—so excessive that, in some cases, it no longer tastes of grapes. It gives the mouth feel you get when you've chewed on a wooden toothpick for too long.

Yeasts. Minute, single-celled fungi that germinate and multiply rapidly as they feed on grape sugars, creating alcohol with the help of enzymes and releasing carbon dioxide. Because different yeasts vary in quality and flavor, winemakers must exercise care in their selection. The yeast cells die after fermentation—after they have run out of food—and slowly drift to the bottom of the wine barrel, where they make up a part of the lees left behind when the wine is racked or filtered.

Zinfandel. A red-wine grape especially popular on the West Coast. Much has been written about its origin, but even though scientists have traced it to an obscure Croatian grape, winemakers agree that the American variety has unique qualities and makes better wine than its European ancestor. Whatever its origin, this grape can give complex, well-balanced wine that ages as well as the best French clarets. It has been planted (and has thrived) in Oregon since the late 19th century, and is currently planted in the Umpqua and Rogue River Valleys.

OREGON VINTAGES

I'm reluctant to supply vintage evaluations, because these work best for small, self-contained districts, such as the Chablis region in France, or Germany's Rheingau. Large, sprawling wine regions, such as those of northwestern Oregon, incorporate too many microclimates with unique conditions ever to allow their wines to be neatly categorized on a definitive vintage chart. Knowing the grower and winemaker and knowing about local conditions is much more important than knowing the vintage.

So as you read these vintage descriptions, keep in mind that they are a rough guide and should never be a substitute for tasting the wine. Even in France, where wineries often lower their prices in off-years, you can find some great wines among a sea of average ones. In other words, once the vintage description has pointed you into a specific direction, you must still visit a winery and sniff, taste, and make up your own mind.

Wines older than the 1994 vintage should have been drunk by now, though a few well-made ones may have survived old age.

1994 Unfortunate weather at bloom made for extremely reduced crop levels, and high temperatures during the harvest caused a rapid rise in sugars. Willamette Valley pinot noirs came in quite ripe, with low acidity, resulting in flabby wines that aged poorly. Southern Oregon reds fared better and are more complex, though these, too, should probably be drunk soon.

1995 Significant rainfall at harvest caused some dilution and rot, but intensive sorting helped create clean and pleasant wines. They're not intense, but they're currently showing a measure of elegance and finesse.

1996 This was a light vintage with higher-than-usual tannins. High acidity levels were responsible for pinot noir with subdued aromas, but southern Oregon reds were big and beautiful. Most of the reds are still on the tannic side and can take a few more years of bottle aging—both cabernet sauvignons and pinot noirs should generally be long-lived wines.

1997 Very high natural crop levels required heavy thinning, and so the wines are light and often watery. Even so, some of the grapes from the Coast Range foothills got quite ripe and are improving with age, and southern Oregon made excellent cabernet sauvignons. Pinot noirs from this vintage contain higher than usual amounts of sediment; decanting is recommended.

1998 This vintage was marked by extremely low crop levels in the Dundee Hills and in the Coast Range foothills, though crop levels were normal in the Eola Hills and in the rest of western Oregon. The grapes came in very ripe, with lower-than-usual acid levels. As a result, the wines matured early, especially those from southern Oregon, and are ready to enjoy now—though some of the bigger reds can improve even further with a few more years of bottle aging.

1999 This was one of the finest vintages in Oregon's wine-growing history, with very complex, beautifully focused wines. The grapes ripened well, yielding wines with excellent structure and multiple layers of flavors, especially the reds of the Umpqua and Rogue River Valleys—though some of the whites, especially pinot blanc and Riesling, can be a tad flat.

2000 A warmer-than-average growing season produced lush fruit and intense wines in the Willamette Valley, though some grapes were caught in late-season rains and made more uneven wines. Both reds and whites are maturing early and may be ready to drink. Umpqua and Rogue River Valley reds, especially malbec, merlot, and tempranillo, are big and bold, with soft but firm tannins, but mellow enough to enjoy now—though they will improve further with more bottle aging.

2001 The fall rains came late in the Willamette Valley, allowing the grapes to ripen fully on the vine. The resulting wines are complex, fragrant, and finely textured. Southern Oregon wines from this vintage are full-flavored and complex, yet surprisingly ready to approach for such young wines. This was an especially fine vintage for pinot gris.

2002 Early releases of pinot gris are on the light side, but the wines might develop more complexity with some bottle age.

I N D E X

COMPASS AMERICAN GUIDES

Compass American Guides are available at special discounts for bulk purchases for sales promotions or premiums. Special editions, including personalized covers, excerpts of existing guides, and corporate imprints, can be created in large quantities for special needs. For more information, write to Special Markets/Premium Sales, 1745 Broadway, MD 6-2, New York, New York 10019, or e-mail specialmarkets@randomhouse.com. Inquiries from Canada should be directed to your local Canadian bookseller or sent to Random House of Canada, Ltd., Marketing Department, 2775 Matheson Boulevard East, Mississauga, Ontario L4W 4P7. Inquiries from the United Kingdom should be sent to Fodor's Travel Publications, 20 Vauxhall Bridge Road, London, England SW1V 2SA.

COMPASS AMERICAN GUIDES

Critics, booksellers, and travelers all agree: you're lost without a Compass.

"This splendid series provides exactly the sort of historical and cultural detail about North American destinations that curious-minded travelers need."
—*Washington Post*

"This is a series that constantly stuns us...no guide with photos this good should have writing this good. But it does." —*New York Daily News*

"Of the many guidebooks on the market, few are as visually stimulating, as thoroughly researched, or as lively written as the Compass American Guide series."
—*Chicago Tribune*

"Good to read ahead of time, then take along so you don't miss anything."
—*San Diego Magazine*

"Magnificent photography. First rate."—*Money*

"Written by longtime residents of each destination...these handsome and literate guides are strong on history and culture, and illustrated with gorgeous photos."
—*San Francisco Chronicle*

"The color photographs sparkle, the archival illustrations illuminate windows to the past, and the writing is usually of the utmost caliber." —*Michigan Tribune*

"Class acts, worth reading and shelving for keeps even if you're not a traveler. "
—*New Orleans Times-Picayune*

"Beautiful photographs and literate writing are the hallmarks of the Compass guides." —*Nashville Tennessean*

"History, geography, and wanderlust converge in these well-conceived books."
—*Raleigh News & Observer*

"Oh, my goodness! What a gorgeous series this is."—*Booklist*

ACKNOWLEDGMENTS

■ From the Author

Many thanks to the winemakers who have welcomed me to Oregon wineries for more than two decades, to Daniel Mangin for walking that extra mile to make sure this book would happen, to Craig Seligman for doing such a great job editing it, to Greg Vaughn for his evocative imagery, and to Fabrizio La Rocca and Tina Malaney for their splendid design work.

■ From the Publisher

Compass American Guides would like to thank Rachel Elson for copyediting the manuscript, Ellen Klages for proofreading it, and Joan Stout for indexing it. Thanks also to Catherine Christenberry for her editorial contributions, to Sarah Felchlin for fact-checking, and to the staff of Moon Street Cartography for assisting with appellations research. We are also grateful to the many wineries that provided us with labels and other materials.

All photographs in this book are by Greg Vaughn unless otherwise noted below. Compass American Guides is grateful to the following individuals or organizations for the use of the photographs or illustrations:

Oregon's Wine History
Page 27, Southern Oregon Historical Society
Page 29, Southern Oregon Historical Society
Page 30 (bottom), Frazier Farmstead Museum
Page 33, Yamhill County Historical Society, Lafayette, Oregon
Page 34, Southern Oregon Historical Society

Food and Wine
Page 40, Dan Wynn © Rita Wynn

Geology: A History of the Soil
Pages 58–59, Oregon Historical Society (Stout 434)

Visiting Wineries

Page 77 (top), Napa Valley Conference Bureau
Page 77 (second and third from top), Forrest L. Doud/Wild Horse Winery
Page 77 (fourth from top), Napa Valley Conference Bureau
Page 77 (fifth from top), Ron Kaplan/Panther Creek Cellars
Page 77 (sixth from top), Marvin Collins, Clos du Val
Page 77 (bottom), Ron Kaplan/Panther Creek Cellars

Washington County

Page 92, Washington County Museum, Portland
Page 100, Montinore Estate

Yamhill County

Page 114, Yamhill County Historical Society

Salem Area

Page 153, Bethel Heights Vineyard

Practical Information

Page 219, David Cooper/Oregon Shakespeare Festival

■ About the Author

John Doerper has worked as a food and wine columnist and editor for numerous publications. His articles about food, wine, and travel have appeared in *Travel & Leisure* and *Pacific Northwest Magazine*, among others. An artist and avid gardener, John is the author of several best-selling Compass American Guides—*California Wine Country, Coastal California, Pacific Northwest,* and *Washington.*

■ About the Photographer

Greg Vaughn's photographs have appeared in *National Geographic, Outside, National Wildlife, Sierra, Natural History,* and *Travel & Leisure,* and he was the principal photographer for Compass *Oregon* and Compass *Washington,* as well as *Washington Wine Country.*